#EMBRACE THE PACE

The 100 Most Exhilarating Lessons Learned in a Decade of Entrepreneurship

BY MATT RIZZETTA

Foreword by Michael D. White

Former Chief Executive Officer, DirecTV; Chief Financial Officer, PepsiCo; Board of Directors, Bank of America, Kimberly-Clark, Whirlpool

TABLE OF CONTENTS

1	DEDICATIONS
3	FOREWORD
5	PROLOGUE
9	Lesson #1: Never Forget the Survival Days
12	Lesson #2: The Man Who Slept in the Conference Room
14	Lesson #3: Take Foul Shots
17	Lesson #4: Losses Equal Learning
19	Lesson #5: Celebrate Winning Moments
21	Lesson #6: Consistency and Longevity Are Overlooked
23	Lesson #7: Develop Championship Habits
25	Lesson #8: The Great Catamaran Ride
28	Lesson #9: The Three Ingredients to Culture
30	Lesson #10: The Golden Rule of Management
33	Lesson #11: Career Cancers Must Be Treated Immediately
35	Lesson #12: Obsess Over the "P" Word
37	Lesson #13: Never Stop Fighting
39	Lesson #14: The Jimmy V Test
41	Lesson #15: The Betting Game
43	Lesson #16: Staying in Business Is a Blessing
45	Lesson #17: Seize the Moments
47	Lesson #18: Youth *Is* a Differentiator
49	Lesson #19: Be a Data Diva
51	Lesson #20: Data Without Discretion is Destruction
53	Lesson #21: Impact Is the Most Valuable Currency

55	Lesson #22: The "Do Something Different" Rule
57	Lesson #23: Fall in Love With the Process
59	Lesson #24: Give a Glimpse, Not a Tour
61	Lesson #25: Promise, Deliver
63	Lesson #26: Listen to Smarter People, Make Your Own Decisions
65	Lesson #27: Let the Competition Fuel You
67	Lesson #28: We Are All Unproven at the Next Level
69	Lesson #29: Make Someone Proud, Prove Someone Wrong
71	Lesson #30: The Org Chart Alignment Test
73	Lesson #31: Results Are the Great Equalizer
75	Lesson #32: Innovation Is Born From Experimentation
77	Lesson #33: Drink Piss and Vinegar and Do Some Crazy Things
79	Lesson #34: Undertrained and Overprepared
81	Lesson #35: Keep It Simple as You Scale
83	Lesson #36: Old School/New School Balance
85	Lesson #37: In Times of Adversity, Lean on Humility and Humor
87	Lesson #38: Juggle the Past, Present and Future
89	Lesson #39: Build an Impenetrable Inner Circle
91	Lesson #40: Enjoy the Curves
93	Lesson #41: How to Destroy the Doubters
95	Lesson #42: Eulogy Over Resume
98	Lesson #43: Lessons From Mom
101	Lesson #44: Look Outside Your Industry
103	Lesson #45: "E" Comes Before "A"
105	Lesson #46: The "It's Not Personal, It's Business" Lie

107	Lesson #47: Find a Safe Haven
109	Lesson #48: Complacency Will Kill Your Career
111	Lesson #49: Proof That Excuses Stink
113	Lesson #50: Be an Energy Addict
115	Lesson #51: The Farm, the Barn and Sunlight
117	Lesson #52: Be "BenSoCal"
119	Lesson #53: Be Patient and Play the Long Game
121	Lesson #54: Always Manage on Offense, Never on Defense
123	Lesson #55: Circle the Two-Jumpers
125	Lesson #56: Grow Thicker Skin
127	Lesson #57: Have a "Stuff Happens" Line on Your P&L
129	Lesson #58: Management by Stimulation Versus Stability
131	Lesson #59: Foresight Gets You Hired, Hindsight Gets You Fired
133	Lesson #60: Bad News Lightspeed Approach
135	Lesson #61: Short-Term Earnings vs. Long-Term Returns
137	Lesson #62: Enter the Lion's Den
139	Lesson #63: Islands Are for Margaritas, Not for Management
141	Lesson #64: Good People Lead You to Great Places
143	Lesson #65: The "SCUSE" Method for Closing Sales
145	Lesson #66: Be the CEO of Your Department
147	Lesson #67: Don't Be Late
149	Lesson #68: Conflict Resolution 101: Fight or Follow-Up?
151	Lesson #69: Be There for Your Teammates
153	Lesson #70: Discipline Is Sexy
155	Lesson #71: Incrementalism Is Sexier
157	Lesson #72: Accountability Is the Sexiest

159	Lesson #73: Always Pay It Forward
161	Lesson #74: You Are Not Self-Made
163	Lesson #75: Control Bucket 3
165	Lesson #76: The SoHo Stroll
168	Lesson #77: The Most Flattering Costs of Doing Business
170	Lesson #78: Keep Mementos by Your Side
172	Lesson #79: Everyone Complains (But Winners Do It With Solutions!)
174	Lesson #80: The Meaning of Money
176	Lesson #81: The Importance of Scenarios and Pressure Testing
178	Lesson #82: Compete and Care
180	Lesson #83: Embrace the Pace
182	Lesson #84: Start and End Strong
184	Lesson #85: I Was Wrong
187	Lesson #86: Championship Months
189	Lesson #87: Do the Little Things
191	Lesson #88: Food Is Nourishing, Meals Are Galvanizing
193	Lesson #89: The Client Value Matrix
195	Lesson #90: The Relationship of Children and Careers
197	Lesson #91: Don't Be Afraid to Ask
199	Lesson #92: Manage to an Outcome, Not to a Message
201	Lesson #93: Mute the Noise
203	Lesson #94: The Cost of People Mistakes
206	Lesson #95: New York, New York
208	Lesson #96: The Difference Between Management and Leadership

210	Lesson #97: Turn to the Outside for First-Time Hires
212	Lesson #98: Don't DiscriminAGE
214	Lesson #99: Unicorns and Clydesdales
217	Lesson #100: 90 Percent Heart, 10 Percent Head
219	CLOSING: "BET ON WALL"
220	The "Bet On" Wall
224	LESSONS TABLE MATRIX
225	END NOTES
225	FOOTNOTE CITATIONS

DEDICATIONS

To my father and mother, who *supported* me through each of these lessons.

To my wife, who *believed* in me through each of these lessons.

To my daughters, who *motivated* me through each of these lessons.

FOREWORD

By Michael D. White

Former Chief Executive Officer, DirecTV; Chief Financial Officer, PepsiCo; Board of Directors, Bank of America, Kimberly-Clark, Whirlpool

When I first met Matt Rizzetta, it was clear that he was a dynamic, innovative young entrepreneur and business leader who had founded and was successfully building a great business. His public relations company, North 6th Agency (N6A), is already one of the top public relations firms in the United States and is one of the top five fastest-growing independent firms. They have a unique approach to measuring and driving real outcomes for their clients. They are also consistently recognized with awards for their unique culture as a Best Place to Work. However, it was also clear that he wasn't satisfied with the status quo. It was evident that Matt was a unique and thoughtful leader in his own right.

With this being the case, I have enjoyed sharing with him my own perspectives, counsel and insights I had acquired throughout my career as an executive at Bain & Company and PepsiCo and CEO of DirecTV.

I have been impressed by Matt's drive, energy and vision to grow his firm, as well as his desire to grow as a leader. I have found him to have an insatiable curiosity and lifelong appetite for learning that is so vital for young entrepreneurs and executives in today's fiercely competitive and fast-changing world.

Over the past years, it has been a pleasure to watch Matt turn into an even stronger leader and put together the building blocks for his vision piece by piece. I have enjoyed our friendship, and it has been gratifying to offer him my perspectives on transactional opportunities, corporate leadership and strategy, which he has applied in his vision to grow N6A. Matt's humility, passion and vision remain a great example for other young entrepreneurs to follow. Little did I realize that Matt is also a great storyteller!

Embrace the Pace: The 100 Most Exhilarating Lessons Learned in a Decade of Entrepreneurship is a journey through the mind of an innovative young entrepreneur who has built something from scratch and is clearly in the process of continuing to build something very unique. It is full of life lessons that he learned from his parents, as well as business insights he picked up in leading N6A. He has learned from other great business leaders, from Ken Langone to Jim Valvano to Jamie Dimon, and shares those insights in the book.

The lessons apply to entrepreneurs, executives and career-minded professionals who are looking to stand out from their peers and reach their potential in the workplace. The lessons capture the essence of true entrepreneurship and the American Dream through stories of perseverance, overcoming adversity and paying it forward. He shares his values and they are firmly grounded in the immigrant experiences of his Italian grandparents.

In my career, I have had the privilege of leading companies that have had an important place in the everyday lives and households of people across the world. I have also been fortunate to work alongside, get to know and learn from some of the greatest business leaders of our time.

I have found that most great leaders share in common a passion for their craft and an insatiable curiosity to learn, as well as humility and a commitment to servant leadership. I am reminded of great leaders such as the late PepsiCo Chief Executive Officer Roger Enrico, under whom I had the privilege of serving as Chief Financial Officer. Roger was among the most transformational corporate leaders of the past century, yet he always felt most at home in a snacks or beverage manufacturing plant, in a grocery store or with a route salesperson, interacting with the people who worked tirelessly on the front lines of the company. He treated everyone equally and never forgot his roots growing up on an iron range in Northern Minnesota.

Many of these same values come through in Matt's lessons. They are values of humility, integrity and hard work, beginning with his decision to name his firm after the street to which his grandparents immigrated and ending with his lesson about the importance of displaying heart and passion for your craft.

I hope you find the lessons to be useful to your professional journey, and I hope you enjoy reading *Embrace the Pace: The 100 Most Exhilarating Lessons Learned in a Decade of Entrepreneurship* as much as I did.

Michael D. White

PROLOGUE

In January 2009, I made up my mind that I was going to start my own business. It was a lifelong goal of mine. I was 26 years old, and soon would be married and expecting my first child. I spent the next 12 months researching, planning and preparing until finally, in January 2010, North 6th Agency, Inc. (N6A) was born.

When I first started N6A, I had read a statistic that indicated only four percent of small businesses survive past the 10-year mark. As soon as I came across this statistic, I made a promise to myself that if I survived 10 years in business, I would write a book to share the most valuable lessons I had learned over the past decade.

So, here I am, 10 years later getting ready to share these lessons and learnings with you.

The first thing I did as soon as I started the business was to name it after the street to which my grandparents immigrated, North 6th Avenue in Mount Vernon, New York. My grandparents arrived in the United States in the 1950s from a poor town in the Puglia region of southern Italy. They never had much. They never spoke our language, never drove a car and never owned a home. Their whole purpose and meaning in life was to set future generations like mine up for success. Although they didn't speak our language, through their sacrifice, hard work and selflessness they managed to communicate to me in a more powerful way than words could ever express.

A decade later, they have a successful business named after them, and one that carries the same values that they taught me. This is something that they could never have dreamed of accomplishing on their own, but more importantly, it is something that I could never have dreamed of doing without their presence and influence.

My only regret is that my grandfather is not here to see it and my grandmother's cerebral capacity has withered away through the effects of dementia. Nevertheless, their influence and spirit live on through my work and through the work of our employees in our company every day.

This is the beautiful part of careers and success. They are always best when they are *shared*.

The journey over the past 10 years has truly been a shared experience in every sense. It has been a journey that wouldn't have been possible without the support, help and compassion of many family members and loved ones, friends, employees, peers and mentors. There have been so many believers who have touched my life and brought a sense of purpose and meaning to my career. I owe so many people a debt of gratitude for making the past decade a truly unforgettable experience. It has also been a journey that wouldn't have been possible without a few doubters along the way. You'll hear about all the lessons I've learned — from the believers as well as the doubters — in the pages ahead.

The past decade has gone by so quickly and brought to life the true meaning of the title of this book, *Embrace the Pace.* It has been exhilarating, stimulating and rewarding beyond my wildest imagination.

A decade later, N6A remains the one and only entrepreneurial venture that I have undertaken in my career other than a failed attempt to start a sports and entertainment agency when I was 22 years old. The journey has required focus, stamina and discipline, but it has been worth it every step of the way.

When I first started the business, I had no idea how much my life would change in the next 10 years. The company has become just as much a part of my life and my legacy as anything. My children have grown up with the company. I've mourned over the deaths of loved ones, rejoiced over the birth of new children, and celebrated weddings, anniversaries and important life events, all under the roof of the company.

The journey has taken me to incredible highs and lows. It has introduced me to great people who have changed my life in many ways. It has changed my life financially. It has changed my outlook and perspectives. It has enriched me with the vibrance, passion and belief shown by everyone who has joined me on the journey.

The journey has challenged me intellectually, emotionally and physically at times. It has stimulated and motivated me in a way that nothing else has. It has brought me great purpose, meaning and sense of accomplishment. It has shown me the beauty of progress, self-improvement and introspection. It has helped me teach invaluable lessons to my three children.

Most importantly, it has shown me the value of *learning*. When it comes to learning, I've done a lot of that over the past 10 years, oftentimes through failures, sometimes through successes and always through mistakes.

Over the years, I've kept a journal of all the lessons that I've learned throughout the journey. Each time I learned a new lesson, I wrote it down in the journal. I've kept the journal for all these years, hoping that we would make it to the 10-year mark so that I could share the lessons with you.

In the pages ahead, I share 100 of the most important of these lessons, with short stories behind each. The lessons are ones of adversity, growth, office relationships, management, leadership, sales and entrepreneurship. In some cases, they are lessons about life that I've learned through the lens of my work.

The lessons are told firsthand by me as a CEO, entrepreneur and founder, but I've found them to apply to all facets of your career, regardless of your job title and regardless of where you are on your career journey. The more I studied these lessons, the more it became evident that they apply to any and all career-minded professionals who are striving to reach their potential in the workplace.

Just like anyone's career, these lessons are a constant work in progress. They are painted on an unfinished canvas that is being worked on continuously.

These are the lessons of the *first* chapter of my career as an entrepreneur.

The same small business survival statistic that indicated only four percent of businesses survive past the 10-year mark indicated that only *one percent* of those businesses are successful at building a global brand over the *next* 10 years.

As proud as I am about beating the odds over the first 10 years, I am even more energized about beating them over the next 10. The road to become one of the one percent of companies that is successful at building a global brand begins now. Just like I did over the first 10 years, my plan is to document all the lessons that I will learn over the next decade. If I'm fortunate enough to beat the odds again, I'll share those lessons 10 years from now. It's a little bit scary to think about. I'll be in my late 40's, and two of my three daughters will be in college.

If the lessons in the next chapter are anything like the ones that I've learned from the first chapter, then I'm in for the journey of a lifetime. I can't imagine anything being as exhilarating as the last 10 years.

I hope you find value in the lessons no matter where you are on your journey, and in some small way they help you in your career in the same way that they've helped me.

I hope you enjoy *The 100 Most Exhilarating Lessons Learned in a Decade of Entrepreneurship.*

#EmbraceThePace

LESSON #1: NEVER FORGET THE SURVIVAL DAYS

I will never forget the afternoon of January 29th, 2010, for as long as I live. It was a Friday leading into a typically frigid New York winter weekend. A 20-year-old artist named Taylor Swift was less than 48 hours away from winning her first Grammy Award, the Winter Olympics were about to commence, and in less than 60 days my first daughter, Viviana, would be born.

But the mood wasn't quite festive where I was that day.

I sat at a booth in a diner on Central Avenue in Yonkers, New York, waiting for my wife to arrive on that cold and gloomy Friday afternoon.

I had just lost my job.

My wife was seven months pregnant.

She had just put in her notice for maternity leave at her job as a teacher at PS 205 in Brooklyn.

We had just closed on our first house and our mortgage payment was due.

We had no income.

The economy was in the depths of a recession.

I had just turned 27, my wife had just turned 30. Only eight months earlier, we had gotten married, and we quickly learned that we were expecting our first child.

Life was a whirlwind, to say the least.

There I sat with my wife at a diner in Yonkers, on Friday, January 29th, 2010, about to ask the scariest question of my life.

Forget about marriage proposals or asking my future in-laws if they would let me marry their daughter. That was a cakewalk compared to the question I was about to ask.

"Will you let me start my own company?" I asked.

The words don't seem so scary now, but back then, in the heat of the moment, I was petrified to ask. The thought of foregoing a stable and steady income to take a Hail Mary risk and start a company with no clients, no money, no connections and no entrepreneurial experience seemed insane. Particularly at that moment in time given where my wife and I were during that stage of our lives.

I had one failed entrepreneurial experience a few years earlier when I was trying to start a sports agency while working a day job simultaneously at Sony BMG. That didn't work out so well, but my wife supported me through it.

I had been working on this business plan for a new kind of public relations firm for the past year, one that brought a different type of energy, approach and culture than other firms. I had been waiting for the right time to take the plunge and go for it. Truth is, in entrepreneurship, there never is a "right time."

I even went so far as to get the business registered a few months earlier, at the tender age of 26: North 6th Agency, Inc. It would be named after the street to which my grandparents immigrated from Italy. I wanted the company to stand for their values. I also wanted it to serve as a constant reminder that I had to "make it" for them. I really wanted to build something meaningful that they could never have built on their own. Not because they weren't smart enough. Simply because they never had the access to resources or the opportunities that I had.

So, there I was, in a Yonkers diner on a cold January afternoon, waiting for my wife to respond to my plea.

My wife, who unlike me is very soft spoken, soothing and understated, gave me her blessing.

"I believe in you," she said. "I know you'll figure out a way to make this work for us."

And with those words, we were open for business and my entrepreneurial journey had officially begun.

As I learned quickly, almost immediately, you're merely in survival mode when you're first starting a business. It is a fight for survival in every sense. Every day you're scratching, clawing and doing whatever you can to survive to fight another day. You're hunting for revenue, defending yourself from falling victim to the competition, and convincing people to come join your no-name company.

Don't let any fancy MBAs or self-professed business savants tell you otherwise. It's not about grandiose vision, disruptive strategy or long-term plans when you're first starting your business.

It's about execution.

It's about survival. Nothing more.

Allow me to let you in on a little secret.

You should *always* be in survival mode. That's how you'll know if you're building a special business or career.

The traits and learnings that are required to make it out of survival mode alive — hunger, scrappiness, speed, discipline and focus, fear of failure (I could go on!) — are traits that will carry you very far at every step of your business or career.

Now, 10 years later, I still carry with me the lessons and memories of those survival mode days and apply them to my day-to-day work life. I never want that to go away. I always told myself that one day, if I ever forgot my survival mode lessons, I would hang it up and look for a new profession. The truth is, we would probably go out of business anyway if we strayed from our survival mode roots.

Each year over the past decade, we've given our staff off the last Friday of every January for N6A Day. It's a way to remember that cold Friday afternoon in January 2010 and the scary question that I popped to my wife in that Yonkers diner.

It's also a way to remember the beginning of our survival days.

A decade later and I still feel like it's survival mode, and I wouldn't want it any other way.

LESSON #2: THE MAN WHO SLEPT IN THE CONFERENCE ROOM

In dealing with people in business, I quickly learned that there is more than meets the eye.

When I first started out in business in 2010, a very successful telecommunications executive named George King was generous enough to offer me free workspace. His office was located at 49 East 52nd Street, a prime location in midtown Manhattan, right across from the iconic BlackRock headquarters.

This was before the days of flexible workspace and co-working giants like WeWork, so it was a major novelty to have an address at a prestigious midtown location. He also let me work out of the space rent-free for a few months, which was a big help to me as I got our business off the ground. Clients and employees in those days were shocked by how impressive our office was. Little did they know I paid nothing for it!

George was a great guy, and I am forever grateful for his generosity to me during those early days of our business. Thanks to him, I was able to keep my overhead down, and have access to a great office with infrastructure already in place such as phones, printers and fax machines (yes, fax machines were still functional back then!).

During these early days, there was another man who was working out of the building. He was introduced to me as an insanely successful Moroccan businessman who had built and exited companies several times over. He had a private penthouse residence on the Upper East Side of Manhattan, he had the backing of many wealthy investors in Europe and Africa, and he had a powerful Rolodex of important business contacts whom he could call upon whenever he needed a favor. After making a fortune, he was now dedicating his life to philanthropy and was using our office as a central hub for his operation to solve world hunger.

After a few weeks of passing each other in the office and exchanging pleasantries by the water cooler, he asked me if I would help him with the marketing and promotion of his cause. He seemed like a nice enough man and his intent was certainly noble, so I said yes. Plus, he was clearly a wealthy and successful businessman, so I could benefit from the networking opportunities that he would provide.

I assisted in him in delivering a few press releases and I shared some of my media contacts to help him spread the word of his mission to the press. Before I knew it, he started asking if I would be willing to offer some of our employees' time to help him promote his mission. We were brand new to business and had just a few employees at the time. Time was precious, but again, it was a good cause and it would provide us with valuable contacts in the business world, so I acquiesced.

A few days later, he excused himself from the office without explanation. He just said he'd be back in a few days. I figured he was traveling overseas to meet with one of his foreign investors. A few days turned into a few weeks. A few weeks turned into a few months. He disappeared, and I never heard from him again.

Months later, when we were preparing to move out of the midtown office and into our new office in TriBeCa — one that we actually paid for! — we cleaned out the conference room. One of our employees noticed something hidden in a nook in the conference table. To this day, I have no idea how he spotted it, as it was buried so deeply in the table you needed superhero vision to have seen it. Sure enough, it was a blanket and a pillow with a change of clothes that belonged to the Moroccan businessman. Everything was so suspect to me, I asked one of our interns to do some digging. It turned out that the Moroccan "businessman" was a total fraud and a scam artist. There was no trace of any successful business exit in his career, and all we could find about his noble "mission" was that he was trying to dupe investors into supporting a faux philanthropic initiative for his own personal gain. The only "penthouse" he had was the floor of our conference room, which he was using as a crash pad because he was broke.

This taught me an important lesson quickly in business. There's always more than meets the eye. This "businessman" saw me as a young impressionable entrepreneur from whom he could receive free labor in an effort to secure funding to feed his own lifestyle, all under the guise of a phony cause-based mission he had created.

There was no Moroccan businessman. There was no penthouse. There was no world hunger mission. All there was was a man who slept in the conference room. And he taught me a valuable lesson about people you meet in business and in your career.

There's always more than meets the eye.

LESSON #3: TAKE FOUL SHOTS

After you read this lesson in its entirety, I think you'll agree that foul shots have changed my career, and they can do them same for yours.

Foul shots are a daily exercise that I developed early in my career, and to this day remain as much a part of my daily routine as brushing my teeth, taking a jog and making myself a morning espresso. Foul shots have enabled me to make some of the most valuable connections, gain exposure to new perspectives, glean inspiration and develop relationships that I never dreamed would be possible. Foul shots have literally changed the entire trajectory of my career.

The concept is pretty simple, and like many other things in my career, draws its inspiration from sports. In basketball, the great players always stay late in the gym, practicing, among other things, taking foul shots.

I remember hearing that Kobe Bryant would stay after practice and refused to leave the gym until he hit 400 shots. He did this every day without exception. The thought being that, over the course of one day, the extra shots he puts up aren't going to make much of a difference. However, with daily repetition, the extra shots will make him a much better player over the course of the year when you count them in *aggregate*.

I decided to adopt this concept into my work routine early in my career. Every day, as soon as I arrived in the office, I would reach out to at least two new people with a personalized message or note, typically via email or phone. The thought being that, over the course of one day, reaching out to two new people wouldn't make much of a difference.

However, with daily repetition, it would make a big impact. Two people each day would equal 10 people per work week. That's 40 people per month. That's nearly 500 people per year. Even if only a small percentage of these people respond to you, you're still meeting somewhere around 50 new people per year, each of them creating new opportunities for you or enriching your career in some way.

Here are some important rules about taking foul shots.

The messages need to be *personalized*, not generic. So, if you read about someone on a blog who piques your curiosity because of a new program he or she has started, the message needs to personalized, referencing the program and other nuanced data points about the person's background. The people to whom you're reaching out need to believe that you've spent the time to research and study them rather than just contact them randomly. They should feel flattered and respected, not like they're being sold to. The intent needs to be genuine and driven by curiosity, not by commercial gain.

The two people to whom you reach out each day could be anybody. Classic foul shot prospects can include people you read about in the news, people you hear about over meals, and people who inspire you or make you curious in some way.

I started doing this exercise when I first began my career as a way to meet new people, build my network and grow as a professional. I estimate that I've taken foul shots to more than 15,000 people in my career. I've probably received responses from 3,000 people or so, which is around a 20 percent response rate. Most importantly, of the 3,000 people who have responded, some have turned into the most valuable relationships and opportunities I've created in my career.

I could share thousands of examples of different foul shots that I've taken and how they've changed the direction of my career, leading me to new revenue opportunities and new growth opportunities and creating jobs and growth opportunities for others. Here's one of my favorites that I share with our staff as an example of why they should take foul shots to get ahead in their careers.

In July 2011, my second daughter, Valentina, was born. A month later, my wife and I took her for her one-month doctor's visit. I sat in the waiting room and picked up a copy of *Westchester Magazine*. In the issue was a feature story about an executive named Aaron Kwittken, who was celebrating his 40th birthday and had achieved great success building a public relations firm.

Being a twentysomething entrepreneur who was aspiring to build something similar to what Aaron had built, the story piqued my interest. I found Aaron's email online and reached out to him with a foul shot, applauding him on his success, introducing myself and inviting him to lunch to get to know him better. He was gracious enough to accept and gave me some great advice when we eventually met. I developed a friendship with Aaron, and from that day we've stayed in touch.

Fast forward a year after the initial lunch meeting, and Aaron introduced me to another executive he knew named Stephen Bradley. Stephen was launching a tech start-up at the time and was looking to hire a public relations firm. Aaron's firm wasn't representing start-ups, but our firm was. Stephen ended up hiring us and we added two new jobs to service Stephen's account, turning the initial foul shot into a revenue-generating and job creation opportunity for our firm.

Pretty cool, huh? But wait, there's more where this foul shot came from!

Three years later Stephen exited his start-up and joined a fast-growing research company named L2. He introduced us to L2's Chief Marketing Officer Katherine Dillon, who ended up hiring our firm. L2 went onto become a flagship client of ours, and we took them through an acquisition to Gartner for more than $100 million.

Through the L2 relationship, I got introduced to their brilliant and high-profile founder Scott Galloway, who has become another friend and supporter of ours. Scott has introduced me to some great clients and contacts through the years, and we actually were presented with a $12 million acquisition offer for our firm as a result of an introduction that Scott had made.

Think about all this for a minute. What started out as a simple foul shot that I took from the waiting room of a doctor's office turned into a nine-year relationship that resulted in new client wins that changed the trajectory of our firm, new revenue-generating opportunities that created jobs and employment growth within our company, and a $12 million opportunity to sell our firm. Most importantly, I count Aaron as a dear friend and great industry peer to this day. I owe him a huge debt of gratitude for responding to my foul shot back in 2011.

If that doesn't validate the value of taking foul shots, I don't know what will.

Trust me on this one. *Take foul shots*. They will change your career.

LESSON #4: LOSSES EQUAL LEARNING

As I look back upon the past decade, it's obvious to me that my greatest learnings have come from losing moments. And there have been too many of those to count.

Whether you're running a business, managing a team of people or simply doing your job every day, you're usually working so hard that you get consumed in the moment. Things are moving so fast and you're constantly being hit with a flurry of good news and bad news. As a result, you're usually onto the next priority before you've had a chance to make time to reflect on the losing moment that you just encountered.

I've found this to be particularly difficult as we've scaled our business. The ability to reflect upon and study losing outcomes from the past has intensified with the size and scale of our operation. However, please hear this loud and clear: You absolutely need to make the time to study your losses.

Over the course of any given week, you're hit with a flurry of losing moments in the workplace. These losing moments can include disappointing outcomes to new business pitches, recruiting candidates who turned you down, botched execution on client work, technical failures and many others. If you're not *learning* from these losing moments then you're missing out on your most valuable opportunities to improve, get better and convert losses to wins the next time around.

I've found time management to be my best friend in my ongoing quest for improvement in this area. The younger version of myself would move so fast and recklessly that I had no regard for time management. Consequently, I never carved out the time that I needed to in order to study losing moments. This caused me to miss out on many opportunities to accelerate our growth. As I've gotten older and more experienced, I've developed a strong appreciation for efficient time management. I've tried to take a more pragmatic approach to make sure the exercise of studying my losses makes it onto my schedule each week without exception.

I find it difficult to learn from the losing moments in the heat of the battle when emotions are running high. So, rather than study the losses in real time, one trick I've picked up over the years is to carve out 10 percent of my time at the end of every week to study this area. Although it requires a level of rigor and discipline, you can always find a few hours each week to study your losses no matter how busy your schedule might be. Even if it means you have to come into the office 15 minutes earlier or leave 15 minutes later, it will be well worth it in the end.

Here's how I've learned to approach my weekly study sessions over the years.

I'll keep a running list of all our losing outcomes as they happen during the week. Then I'll solicit quick feedback from other managers who have had a hand in the outcomes. I'll jot down their perspectives, insights and feedback. I've found their insights to be incredibly valuable and equip me with the necessary data points that I need when studying the losses each week. Then on Friday morning, I'll come into the office extra early and spend 90 minutes studying each outcome, reviewing feedback from managers, and writing down potential solutions to convert the losses to wins next time around.

This allows me to create distance between the losing moments themselves and enables me to study the outcomes with a clear head and an objective mindset.

Why did we lose that new business pitch? Who did we lose to and what could we have done better? What was the feedback from the prospect? Why didn't we land our top recruiting candidate? Was it over money, culture or something else? What could we have done better? How can we get that candidate the next time around?

These are the questions that I've learned to ask myself during my weekly sessions when I study our losing outcomes.

The 10 percent of my time that I've spent studying losses has led to our greatest improvements as a company and my greatest improvements as a manager and leader. It has become among the most valuable time blocks on my schedule each week.

Losses equal *learning*. Make the time to study them. I wish I had learned this lesson much earlier in my career.

LESSON #5: CELEBRATE WINNING MOMENTS

There is no better feeling than being a part of a winning team, and the workplace is no exception. When I look back at the last decade, perhaps no quote sums up my feelings toward winning more than this one from former Starbucks CEO Howard Schultz:

"Success is best when it's shared."

My greatest enjoyment has come from winning moments that have been shared and celebrated with others.

While it sounds like such a simple concept, it actually has been a major challenge for me. In fact, while we've done our fair share of celebrating over the years, I regret not finding more time to rejoice in winning moments when they've happened. We've had so many reasons to celebrate over the years, such as achieving important business milestones, winning new business pitches over larger competitors, reaching revenue goals, winning national awards and recognitions, and announcing employee promotions and leadership accomplishments.

Too often I've squandered opportunities to celebrate these milestone moments because I was already onto the next thing on my checklist.

Just like I've found it to be difficult to make time to study and learn from losing moments (see "Lesson #4: Losses Equal Learning"), I've found it equally as challenging to make time to celebrate the winning moments.

What you don't realize is that, when you miss these opportunities, you're missing your best chances to create valuable bonds, build chemistry and create galvanizing moments with your team.

At times, I've even felt like I was too "cool" to rejoice in winning moments. In my own mind, I felt that by rejoicing in them I would somehow send the wrong signal that winning was unexpected in our organization, or that it would jinx us the next time around. All of that was *dead* wrong.

If you're managing a team, winning moments can create a feeling of electricity and energy unlike anything else in the workplace. Winning is contagious, and everyone wants to be a part of it. Who doesn't like to be a part of a winning team, and who doesn't like to celebrate the feeling of winning together?

You should encourage high fives in the office for doing great work for tricky clients. Don't be afraid to take your team out to an impromptu meal after you hit your goals for the month. Don't hold back from blasting your sales representative's favorite song through your speakers after they close those big deals.

You might not see it at the time, but these are all opportunities for you to create a culture where winning is seen as a uniting force for everyone to rejoice in. It will also make the losing moments that much more piercing. By extension, this will create a culture where there is a curiosity and thirst for learning when you lose because your people are so hungry to win.

When you're running a business, it's hard to celebrate to the extent that you would like. You're constantly worried about all the pressures and stresses that come with managing the day-to-day operation.

How can you possibly celebrate that account you just closed or that junior staffer's promotion when you have cash flow on your mind or aging receivables to worry about? Well, you need to remind yourself that *you* are the tempo-setter for the organization. It's just as much a part of your job to set the precedent for how the organization celebrates winning moments as it is to worry about the rest of the operation.

Do you want your organization or team to be seen as one that is ho-hum about winning, or one that celebrates and shares in the feeling of winning?

After making many mistakes over the years, I know exactly which side of that equation I would choose to be on.

Give me that winning feeling. There's *no* other feeling like it in the workplace.

LESSON #6: CONSISTENCY AND LONGEVITY ARE OVERLOOKED

When I first started our business, I was an impatient and naive twentysomething with a misguided sense of what success was all about. I've kept the initial business plan that I built for N6A when I was 26 years old, and from time to time I'll look at it and laugh. It's funny to me, because these were the superlatives that I used to define success in our business plan back then: "immediate," "instant," "sprint."

Back then, success to me was nothing more than a sprint to see how fast I could make it, how big I could build it, and how disruptive I could be in the shortest amount of time.

In reality, elements of this probably contributed to our early success and survival during our formative years as a business. However, I've learned that these are hollow, shortsighted and unfulfilling principles that are the furthest thing from making you a success in your career.

When I evaluate myself today as a business leader and when I meet with people of all walks, including entrepreneurs, founders, CEOs, prospective employees and entry-level youngsters, I am no longer interested in overnight success stories. I am no longer interested in instant gratification or fast-tracking the road to success. I am much more interested in two words:

Consistency and *longevity*.

These are perhaps the two most overlooked qualities in one's career.

Anyone can be a one-hit wonder — just ask Milli Vanilli or Fountains of Wayne (I'm dating myself now!). I'm no longer impressed by one-hit wonders who boast of quick success or have achieved overnight stardom. But find me someone who can churn out Top 40 hits consistently, year after year, and now we're talking.

Over the past 10 years, I've seen many people in my network strike gold. Some of these people remain close friends of mine to this day. Many of them were in the right place at the right time, riding the waves of tech booms, perfectly timed venture capital windows and bull markets. I would never take anything away from their accomplishments. In fact, many of them have an innate ability and vision which I could never dream of having. However, while they've had successful outcomes, I wouldn't necessarily call their *careers* a success.

As I've gotten deeper into my business and career journey, I have seen that the true success stories are the ones whose careers are defined by *consistency* and *longevity*. These are people who have achieved sustained success over long periods of time, oftentimes reinventing themselves in order to constantly churn out winning outcomes year after year. They might not have experienced some of the big wins over the short term that others have, but over the long term they've achieved consistent success without many blips.

Case in point: I can name hundreds, maybe thousands, of people in my network who have had successful financial exits in a relatively short horizon. These are people who have struck gold quickly and got out at the right time.

However, I can name only a handful of people in my network who have achieved consistent winning outcomes, year after year. By winning outcomes, I don't necessarily mean financial outcomes, although that is one metric for determining success. Beyond financial outcomes such as profitability, shareholder returns or valuation increases, winning outcomes in your career could mean other things, such as employment creation, promotion rates, product innovation, customer success track record and impact on others. To me, those are the true "one-percenters," and the ones who embody what it means to have a successful career.

As I look back at the decade we've been in business, I wouldn't say we've ever had one grand-slam year. However, we've had 10 consecutive winning years of consistent profitability, innovation, job creation, improvement and growth. I don't think that I appreciated this as much as I should have in the early days, but nowadays I'm very proud of our track record when it comes to consistency and longevity.

When all is said and done, I want my career and business journey to be remembered for consistency and longevity, and I'm fine with it even if it comes at the expense of short-term gratification.

My ideology around success has changed quite a bit since I was an impatient and naive twentysomething.

LESSON #7: DEVELOP CHAMPIONSHIP HABITS

As an avid sports fan, I always found it to be cliché whenever a coach would talk about championship habits. What does that even mean? Are there such habits that makes one team successful and another team unsuccessful?

Clearly there was no substance behind this, right? I always felt this was nothing more than coach-speak whenever I heard it.

Until I started our business.

That's when I realized that there really are habits that separate average teams from championship teams. In no particular order, here are 10 habits I've noticed our most winning employees, customers and peers have had in common over the years.

1. *Always be on time.* Championship players rarely show up late for meetings.

2. *Get into a routine.* This is usually a reflection of someone's discipline and focus in the workplace.

3. *Be efficient with your time.* Look at the ones who are doing the most with their time, not necessarily spending the most time in the office.

4. *Anticipate questions before they're asked.* The ability to anticipate the needs of the customer and peer is usually a sign of someone's instinct and discretion.

5. *Manage by walking.* Getting up and walking around the office versus sitting behind a desk all day will tell you a lot about someone's ability to manage people.

6. *Communicate verbally, not just from behind a computer.* Emails and texts play an important role in management. Just not 100 percent of the time.

7. *Don't avoid confrontation.* The ones who face confrontation head-on and with a solutions-oriented mindset are championship players.

8. ***Don't talk over people.*** *This is a sign of social disconnect and a need to always be in control.*

9. ***Be a better listener than talker.*** *Good talkers are a dime a dozen. Good listeners are rare and unique.*

10. ***Support arguments with analytics.*** *The ones who present data to support their arguments are usually the most diligent, logical and sensible on the team.*

In all of my years working alongside colleagues and being exposed to talent of all shapes and sizes, I've noticed that the most successful ones have many of these habits in common.

If you're looking to build a championship team in the workplace — one that continuously wins and improves — I would look to hire people with as many as these habits as possible. It's almost impossible to find someone who possesses all of these qualities, but in aggregate you want to surround yourself with a team that checks all of these boxes across the organization. While it's hard to vet for many of these during the interview process, you can usually ask questions that will give you a good indication of whether or not the candidate possesses championship habits.

"Talk to me about your daily routine. What's an example of how you would manage your time when juggling these three priority tasks?"

"If you're managing someone, how do you determine which communication method to use?"

"What is your approach to handling confrontation in the office?"

"Where would you rank your listening skills compared to your speaking skills?"

These are the types of questions I've learned to ask in order to determine whether candidates possess championship habits.

It took me almost a decade to realize it, but I must confess that championship habits are more than just coach-speak.

LESSON #8: THE GREAT CATAMARAN RIDE

In January 2015, I took a trip with my wife to Hawaii. I was there to attend a trade show and meet with the management team of a large client whose account we were pursuing (you can read more about this meeting in "Lesson #87: Do the Little Things").

My wife joined the trip, and we had planned to use the rest of the week following the prospect meeting to enjoy some quality time to ourselves in Hawaii. Between the demands of running a business over the past five years and of raising three young children, my wife and I hadn't taken a real vacation in several years. This would finally be our chance to get away and relax a little bit without any distractions.

We flew in on Sunday. The prospect meeting was booked for Tuesday, so the plan was to prepare all day on Monday, attend the meeting on Tuesday, and then we would have the rest of the week to ourselves to enjoy the beautiful Hawaiian Islands. The prospect meeting went well, and I was looking forward to spending some much-needed alone time with my wife. The first thing we did was book a catamaran trip.

The setting for the catamaran trip was picturesque. It was a gorgeous Hawaiian morning, the sun was glistening, ukulele music was playing soothingly in the background, and a mouthwatering cocktail was in our hands. I took a deep breath, exhaled and was ready to go into vacation mode.

It was the perfect way to kickstart the vacation part of the trip.

Only we never made it to the "vacation" part.

The catamaran wasn't even 500 feet offshore yet when my phone rang. It was one of our clients attending the trade show. He was a good friend of mine and he ran a company for which I served as a board member. My wife's look said it all. It was one of the looks she gives me when I should absolutely *not* pick up my phone, even though she knows I'm going to pick it up anyway. She had been with me long enough to know that I was going to pick up the phone. I always picked up whenever a client called.

"Sorry, babe," I said. "I have to pick this up."

The client was in a panic. "Matt, I'm *really* sorry to do this to you," he said. "Somehow I double-booked myself and I need you to give the opening speech on the Internet of Things at noon today on the conference stage."

"Of course," I said. "Whatever you need."

I hung up and took a big gulp. A speech! Not just any speech, but he asked me to deliver the opening speech to a packed audience of telecommunications and technology executives on a topic that I had absolutely no knowledge of.

"How the hell am I going to give a speech in three hours to a large audience of technology executives on the Internet of Things?" I thought to myself.

The Internet of Things (IoT) might as well have been about neuroscience and complex algorithmic formulas. It would have meant the same to me. I knew absolutely nothing about IoT at the time other than how to promote companies that offered IoT services.

My wife looked at me with a sign of resignation. She knew me well enough to know what was coming next.

"Stop the boat!" I exclaimed. "I need to get off the boat!"

The catamaran captain stopped the boat but proceeded to tell me that they were too far offshore to turn around. So, I jumped off the boat, right into the Pacific Ocean. The water was almost up to my head. I held my mobile phone above my head and waded all the way back to shore. It was a crazy thing to do, and the other couples who were on the boat definitely thought my wife was married to a lunatic.

After I dried off and got dressed at the hotel, I spent the next few hours reviewing data points and getting a crash course on all things IoT-related. I wasn't going to turn into an IoT expert in three hours, but at least I needed to sound like I knew *something* about the topic.

Three hours later I was on stage, giving the opening speech on the future of IoT. I was so nervous that I was going to sound like an incompetent idiot. I needed to do something to break the ice and get the crowd on my side early on.

"Up until three hours ago I didn't know much about IoT, but I could tell you a *hell* of a lot about Hawaiian catamarans," I said.

I then proceeded to tell the entire story of the catamaran ride, the dive off the boat, and how I arrived on stage to speak about IoT. The audience cracked up, and it put me at ease for the next 30 minutes.

The speech turned into a fun, interactive and open forum session about marketing and public relations for IoT companies — a topic that I actually did know something about! I wasn't a domain expert on IoT by any means, but I certainly knew a thing or two about how to promote and market it. Even though I was terrified three hours earlier, it turned out to be an enjoyable experience and a great memory in my career.

The catamaran experience and keynote speech taught me a valuable lesson about how to prepare for something on a moment's notice. Lean on things like humor, self-deprecation and candor when you're asked to do something on a whim.

I owe my wife another catamaran ride, and a real Hawaiian vacation this time.

LESSON #9: THE THREE INGREDIENTS TO CULTURE

I'm asked a lot about culture whenever I meet with clients, prospects and candidates. It's probably the area of accomplishment that I'm most proud of when I look back at my first 10 years of entrepreneurship. We've been fortunate enough to have won all sorts of great awards and accolades recognizing our culture, including being named *PR Week*'s Best Places to Work, *Digiday*'s Most Innovative Culture and *Entrepreneur*'s Top Company Cultures in America.

I'm most proud of this because it's something we work on tirelessly. Strong culture is something that should always be an unfinished mosaic for a company. It constantly needs to be refined and improved and requires the contributions of many artists, not just one.

Whenever I take clients and prospects out to dinner, they always ask me about our "secret" to creating a great company culture. The truth is, behind great culture is great discipline and an unglamorous process that includes constant effort, rigorous solicitation of feedback, and ongoing checks and balances. If you're not hitting the road with employees, asking them questions, taking them out to breakfasts and lunches, and soliciting feedback on areas for improvement, you're never going to make any progress improving your culture and making it stand out from your competitors.

Beyond the unglamorous processes above, I've found that truly great company culture boils down to three things:

Consistency, authenticity and differentiation.

Allow me to explain each.

Consistency. Have you ever applied for a job or inquired about a company because it seemed like a great place to work, but when you showed up in person it was a totally different experience than what you'd heard about or read about online? This is a major red flag in the culture test. Consistency between a company's online portrayal of their culture and the feeling you get when you see it in action is usually a sign that a company's culture is stable and strong. On the other hand, if the company represents their culture one way online but you can sense it's different once you step off the elevator, it likely means that they don't have a real vision or identity when it comes to their people.

Authenticity. The true barometer of strong culture is authenticity and genuineness. People should want to be a part of a *real* culture. Something that is true, genuine and is clear about the values for which the company stands. There is usually a direct link between authenticity and empathy, and empathy is fast becoming the most critical buzzword around the water cooler. Even if you don't necessarily agree with everything, do you believe the company is authentic and stands behind its core principles? If so, chances are the company has an authentic culture rather than one that is contrived and struggling to find an identity.

Differentiation. Ultimately, if you're going to create any type of meaningful culture, you're going to have to do some things differently. Nobody ever created a special culture by playing copycat alone. When you look at the company's culture, ask yourself if what it is doing is original, unique and innovative, or if it is simply putting a different stroke on a page from the playbooks of others. Of course, some elements of the company's culture should reflect learnings from other successful companies. However, if the company isn't doing anything that is differentiated or original with their culture, it means they're not putting in the time or effort its people deserve.

Culture can be a very abstract topic, but when it's broken down into its simplest form, I would say the recipe to a winning culture includes an equal dosage of three ingredients: *consistency, authenticity and differentiation.*

LESSON #10: THE GOLDEN RULE OF MANAGEMENT

If you're a first-time manager, you should pay extra close attention to this lesson.

I've spent a considerable amount of time over the past decade thinking about the one rule of management that I would encourage first-time managers to espouse. The conclusion I've drawn is that I'm not sure there is one golden rule that applies to all management relationships, but this one is pretty damn close.

Avoid surprises.

This is so important that it's worth repeating.

Avoid surprises.

The very first thing you should do as a first-time manager is sit your direct reports down and tell them the following: Their job is to make sure you are never surprised. Your job is to give them all the tools they need to make sure you are never surprised.

I've been through all sorts of uncomfortable situations with my direct-report team through the years. Even though some of these situations have been trying and even cringeworthy at times, I've found that we can overcome pretty much anything together. I have yet to find one example of an uncomfortable situation between my direct reports and me that was unfixable.

Workplace romances? I've heard about them.

Lawsuit threats from fake-tough-guy clients? I've picked up those calls.

Obscene office behavior? I've seen it on display.

No-show employees? I've held the elevator all day waiting for them.

Cybersecurity attacks? I've been the recipient.

Inebriated happy hour games? I've closed my eyes and pretended I didn't see it.

You name it and I've seen it all at this point.

In time, I've learned that I can pretty much handle any type of bad news and whatever collateral damage might come with it. However, there is one catch when it comes to bad news.

You should never be surprised.

Chances are, as a manager, you can handle that Johnny Customer is not happy and might fire you. However, what you can't tolerate is that Johnny Customer is not happy and you *didn't know* about it. That's where you must draw the line in the sand if you're a manager. It should never get to that point. The job of your subordinates is to prepare you so that you're never surprised.

If you have one non-negotiable rule as a manager, this should be it. Your subordinates should know that you can get through any type of sticky situation with them no matter how ugly it is. However, you should never be surprised.

Perhaps a client is not happy with your team's service. You can deal with the issue; you just can't be blindsided by it.

Maybe your sales team is going to lose that big new business pitch they worked so hard for. You can replace the deal; you just can't be surprised by the outcome.

Perhaps Employee A is giving Employee B a problem. You can figure out a solution; you just can't be surprised about it.

As long as you can prepare for bad news, you can make the necessary adjustments to recover from it. It's when you get blindsided by news that you weren't prepared for that you get into real trouble.

Whenever I bring somebody onto my direct-report team, the first rule I go over with them is this one. *Avoid surprises.*

"We can get through anything together," I tell them. "Just make sure that I'm never surprised."

You should have a wonderful working relationship with your subordinates where you support each other, you lift each other up and you enjoy winning together. However, under no circumstances should you tolerate being surprised with bad news.

As a manager, you should *never, ever, ever* be surprised with news you weren't prepared for.

This rule should get handed down to all levels of the organization. So, if it's incumbent on the CEO's direct reports to avoid surprises, the CEO's direct reports need to hold their subordinates to that same standard, and so on.

When you build a management supply chain where every level of the organization views it as their responsibility to make sure there are no surprises at the level above them, you create an incredibly potent combination of accountability and pride of ownership.

Let's say it one more time to make sure the point gets across.

Avoid surprises.

This the closest thing there is to a golden rule of management.

LESSON #11: CAREER CANCERS MUST BE TREATED IMMEDIATELY

Here's a lesson that I learned early on in business.

Cancers will kill your career or business if they're not treated *immediately*.

Let me tell you a quick story about how I learned this lesson the hard way.

When we were just starting to scale our business back in 2010, we hired a young employee who was a problem child. The employee was a solid producer but was quick to badmouth me, disrespect his managers and talk negatively about our vision to our entry-level newbies.

It was evident that this employee had not bought into working at our company and thought he was doing us a favor by gracing us with his presence in the office every day. The employee had no problem voicing his concerns to subordinates at the water cooler rather than discuss them openly behind closed doors.

It was clear that the employee was becoming a cancer to our culture.

However, this employee was a strong producer. In fact, he quickly became one of our top producers. Additionally, we were just getting started out in business, so it was difficult for me to recruit talent. At that time, it was tough to find talent who wanted to come work for a no-name start-up that was run by a founder who had no real business experience or track record to speak of. Rather than fire the employee, I chose to look the other way. I allowed the toxic behavior to continue.

That was a *huge* mistake.

Not surprisingly, a few months later the employee resigned.

Then one of our fast-rising entry-level employees resigned.

Then *another* one resigned.

Now I had a full-fledged talent crisis on my hands.

With this, I quickly found out why toxic cultural hires were so cancerous.

They weren't cancerous because of the *immediate* impact that they had on our business. They were cancerous because of the *generational* impact they had on *others*.

Allow me to explain.

I clearly wasn't upset when the cancerous employee resigned. In fact, I was somewhat relieved. However, when we started to lose promising and perfectly levelheaded young talent, that's when I really started to feel the burn. These youngsters were future stars. They were all managers and leaders of tomorrow and A-plus players, as I saw them. And now they were all gone for good.

I could understand why the cancerous employee left, but why were we losing these other young employees who had just chosen to launch their careers with our company a few months earlier?

I totally underestimated the influence that the cancerous employee had on the others. Truth is, I should've known better. Young talent is very impressionable and many times they don't know better. In their minds, the cancerous employee was *right.* As a result of the cancerous employee's influence, the young talent felt that they *were* working for a no-name start-up with an incompetent CEO who had a dead-end vision. With a direct line to the cancerous employee, I should have realized that the young future stars would be more influenced by the problem person than by me or anyone else on our senior leadership team.

It took me a long time to recover from this. The search for replacements lasted a few months, not to mention all the valuable opportunity costs that I left on the table along the way. Had I just acted quickly and removed the cancer immediately, I would have saved lots of time, I would have been able to redirect my focus in growth areas for our business and, most importantly, I would have retained promising talent that could be running offices for us today.

Chances are, if there's a toxic employee on your team, his or her influence will quickly spread to others on the team just like a cancer would. You'll quickly find that once-promising talent will now be corrupted and infected in a way that they never would have if you had simply removed the cancer in the first place.

This was an important lesson I learned early on. Career cancers will kill you not because of the *immediate* impact they have, but because of the *generational* impact they will have on others.

If you have a cancer on your team, don't wait. Treat it immediately. Trust me on this one. Do it for the future generations.

LESSON #12: OBSESS OVER THE "P" WORD

In May 2015, I was asked by my alma mater Iona College to join its Board of Directors. It was a real honor for me. It was also somewhat surreal seeing as how less than a decade earlier, I was sitting in a classroom without any real sense of direction or vision for my career. Now Iona was asking me to join the board.

As a first order of business as a board member, the college asked me to come in and speak to students in its business school. I was 10 years into my career and five years into my business at that time.

I drove out to campus and spent an hour speaking to students about everything and anything I could think of that had shaped me since my career had begun — people I had met, lessons I had learned, tips and best practices I had picked up from firsthand experience. You name it, I spoke about it.

The students seemed to enjoy it, but after the speech was over, one student came up to me. "Mr. Rizzetta" the student asked. "Of all the things you spoke about today, what is the one word you would use to define success in your career?"

I was totally speechless.

It was such a simple and straightforward question, but truth is that I had no answer for it in that moment.

There I was, fresh off of giving an hourlong speech sharing words of advice and real-world experiences of growing a business, yet I couldn't answer the most simple and basic question that a student asked. I was pretty embarrassed and ashamed actually.

"I need to think about that," I told the student. "Let me get back to you."

I'm usually very diligent with follow-up, but I didn't follow up with the student for almost three years. That's not to say that I hadn't thought about his question. In fact, I had thought about it quite regularly. The truth is, I just didn't have an answer for it.

What is the one word that defines a successful career?

Almost four years later, I found the student on LinkedIn and sent him a note. He was now a second-year accountant on Wall Street and well into his own career journey by that point.

We were coming up on a decade in business and I had been doing a lot of thinking and reflecting during that period of time. I finally found the word that had escaped me all these years.

"Progress," I titled the subject line of the LinkedIn message.

"That's the word I couldn't think of when you asked me that question several years back."

I had no idea if this guy was going to remember that conversation, or even if he was going to remember me at all for that matter. But I finally found my answer to his question and I wanted to share it with him.

It took me a long time to realize this, many years in fact. But ultimately, I've come to realize that success in your career should be defined by the progress you make. I think back to my own career journey, and any success I've experienced is nothing more than the result of making incremental progress. What progress have I made as a manager? What progress have I made as a leader? As a mentor? As a CEO? As a decision maker? As a member of the community?

I look back at mistakes I made earlier in my career and I think to myself: How on earth could I have been so stupid?

If you're not constantly making progress then you're not reaching your potential. And success ultimately comes down to fulfilled potential. I am 37 years old now. I know for certain when I look back at 47, 57, 67 and so on, the progress I made (or didn't make) will be the main barometer to determine my own definition of success in my career.

We all have different definitions of potential. But we all have the same definition of progress, and we are in full control of whether we make it or not. The more progress we make, the closer we come to reaching our potential.

If there's one word to obsess over in your career, it's the "P" word.

Progress.

Thank you to the student at Iona College who helped me come to this realization. It only took four years.

LESSON #13: NEVER STOP FIGHTING

In the early 2000s, when I was still in college, I competed as an amateur boxer. This culminated in March 2005 when I found myself in the Copacabana on the west side of Manhattan, competing in the quarterfinals of the New York Golden Gloves, the most prestigious amateur boxing competition in the state.

I was just two fights away from making it to Madison Square Garden, the most legendary arena in the world, for a chance to win the Golden Gloves title in my weight class. I had a sizable cheering section of family and friends, all of whom traveled far and wide to watch me fight. I had trained so hard for the fight: an intense, six-month regimen of daily jogging sessions at 5 o'clock in the morning, ring training and sparring battles at Morris Park Boxing Gym in the Bronx, and a maniacally strict diet of egg whites, fruit and water. All of the sacrifices from the prior six months were finally going to pay off for me on that night. I was convinced that I was going to win and I would go onto Madison Square Garden for a chance to win it all.

Then it all ended in one minute and 47 seconds. I had been knocked out, ruled out by a standing eight count from the referee. My dream of competing at Madison Square Garden was over in less than the amount of time it took to listen to a Missy Elliott song (she was at the top of charts that year). So was my boxing career.

That was the last time I ever stepped foot inside of a boxing ring. Three months later, I graduated from college, started my career and left behind my boxing dreams for good.

It's been almost 20 years since that knockout loss in the Golden Gloves, but some of the most valuable lessons that I've carried with me in my career to this day come from my experience in a boxing ring.

The most important one? *Never stop fighting*.

Just like in boxing, in your career the *outcome* is never in your control, but the *effort* always is. As disappointed as I was that I lost the fight that night — I still think about it to this day — I am proud that I never gave up. I made the sacrifices, put in the daily effort and work required, and fought until the bitter end when the referee ruled me out.

I've had much bigger and more significant losses in my business career than I did in my boxing career. Through it all, I've learned to never stop fighting. I will always get up for the next round. So far, unlike in my boxing career, there has yet to be a referee who has counted me out in business and told me the fight was over.

I'm not proud of all the outcomes that I've produced in my career, and I've been far from a perfect person at times, but I am proud that I have never stopped fighting through it all. I know for a fact that, if I had stopped fighting at times, my entire career trajectory would have turned out differently. I probably would have given up on business much sooner. I likely would have stopped trying to scale when it became painfully stressful. I also have the same commitment to my direct reports. I will never let them stop fighting, no matter how difficult it gets at times.

Who would've thought that one of the most valuable lessons I would learn in my business career would come from a minute-and-47-second knockout punch in a boxing ring? But in fact, it did.

Maybe that punch didn't hurt so much after all. *Never stop fighting.*

LESSON #14: THE JIMMY V TEST

As I continue through my career journey, *who* I surround myself with has become increasingly more important to me than *what* I am surrounded by. It's the *people* more than the *things* that I've learned to care about as I've gotten deeper into my career.

Who would've ever thought that being such a big college basketball junkie would lead me to learn one of the most important management lessons of my career?

Legendary coach and champion for cancer survivors Jim Valvano ("Jimmy V") once famously stated that a complete day should include each of the following:

A moment of *laughter.*

A moment of *thought.*

A moment of *tears.*

I've been blessed through the years to work with some incredible people, and people for whom I have deep respect and admiration.

Although it took many years to get to this point, I have a very special bond with the people I surround myself with in the workplace, particularly those who report directly to me.

Long ago, as I was starting to build my team, I started to use the three tenets of Jimmy V's monologue to guide me on personnel decisions. From that point forward, I started referring to the Jimmy V tenets to determine who would make it into my inner circle.

Is this someone I can *laugh* with?

Is this someone who will move me to *thought?*

Is this someone who I'm comfortable showing emotion in front of?

It might seem overstated, but the truth is that you spend more time with your colleagues than you do with many friends and family members. You go through life with these people just as much as with anyone. Just like life, your career includes many emotional arcs, such as laughter, thought and hardship.

You should strive to become the most complete version of yourself inside the office as you strive to become the most complete version of yourself as a person outside the office.

If you're going to accomplish anything of significance in your career, it's going to require sacrifice, gut-wrenching decisions and the ability to push beyond your limits at times.

Why wouldn't you choose to surround yourself with people who will push you to be the best version of yourself? In order to do this, I've learned to surround myself with people at work who are capable of evoking the same emotions that my friends, companions and life partners are.

When you think about who you want to surround yourself with in your career, ask yourself if they evoke these emotions. If that seems too extreme, you should at least ask yourself if you would be comfortable laughing, thinking and crying in front of them. If the answer is no, you should rethink whether they're worth placing in your inner circle. If the answer is yes, then you've found a special one.

Laugh, think, cry. These are such basic human emotions that have led me to develop the most special bonds of my career.

Thank you, Jimmy V. Rest in peace.

LESSON #15: THE BETTING GAME

The deeper I get into my career, the more evident it becomes that my professional journey is nothing more than a series of bets that I've made on people. The same can be said by anyone who has crossed my path along his or her professional journey. These people have made a bet on me and my company, and it is my responsibility to make sure that bet pays off for them in the end.

It's important to understand the betting culture as you continue to navigate through your career.

Employees bet on companies to advance their careers, companies bet on employees to advance their businesses, customers bet on providers to fulfill their service demands. The crazy workforce we are all navigating through is nothing more than an ecosystem of bets that we are making on each other.

This might seem like an emotionless, platonic and transactional philosophy, but that's not the case. Smart bets on the right people and the right companies will bring a harmony like you've never felt before in your career. When you've made a good bet on a person in your career, you should keep your money on the winner. When you've made a losing bet on a person, you should cut your losses quickly and move on.

The greatest sense of accomplishment in my career has come from winning bets I've made on people. Of course, when you're in business for a decade, you're inevitably going to make some losing bets as well. Here are some signs that you're betting on winning people in your career:

See how your peers handle defining moments. Inevitably, you will be exposed to what I refer to as "defining moments" alongside your peers over the course of your career. These moments tend to be personal in nature just as much as they are work-related. How did your manager handle things when you celebrated a life event? How did your subordinate react when you were dealing with a death in the family? How your co-workers handle defining moments is a good barometer of whether you've made a bet on the right people.

Choose smart losers over sore losers. Over the course of your relationship with peers in the workplace, you're going to lose together just like you're going to win together. Lost customers, botched execution, mishandled strategy. You're human, so these things are going to happen. The important thing is to surround yourself with *smart* losers, not *sore losers*. Think back to the losing moments. Were your co-workers smart losers who learned and improved as a result or did they pout over the losses? If you're with smart losers, chances are you're betting on the right people.

Envision the payoff stage. Every bet has an expiry. Regardless of whether it's short-term or long-term, ask yourself what the payoff stage looks like when the bet you made on a person is over. This is a good question to determine if you've made a winning bet on the right people in your career. Can you envision that person leading you to better places in your career? Can you envision yourself reaching new heights with that person? Do you see that person as someone with whom you want to progress in your career? Understand the bet you're making on that person, the shelf life of the bet and what you think it looks like at the payoff stage. If there is a smile on your face when you think of the payoff stage, then you've picked a winner. If there's a frown when you think of the payoff stage, then cut your losses now.

This is the betting game that we all play in our careers. Bet wisely.

LESSON #16: STAYING IN BUSINESS IS A BLESSING

On the walk into my office every day I am reminded of the significance of staying in business. *Literally.*

Our office is located in the chic SoHo neighborhood in downtown Manhattan. The neighborhood is the epicenter of the world when it comes to high-end fashion boutiques, trendy yoga studios and fresh-pressed pomegranate kale juice stands. Admittedly, we have strayed quite far from our blue-collar roots in our selection of office space. However, I remember dreaming of being able to afford an office of this caliber when we first started our business, so I was happy to splurge when we moved into this space in the summer of 2017.

Every morning, I park my car in a garage on West Broadway near Grand Street, which serves as a sort of unofficial gateway to SoHo. After I make a final turn off Canal Street, with its knockoff sunglass vendors, "I Love NY" t-shirt stands and dollar pizza shops, the luxury and privilege of SoHo hits me like the Vegas Strip.

The walk from the garage to the office is just four short blocks, but it serves as a reminder of the fragility and unpredictability of running a business.

As I make my way up West Broadway, storefront after storefront is boarded up. Once fine establishments like family-owned cafes, well-funded restaurants and ambitious retailers are now out of business. Most of these are businesses that were once thriving and are now unable to afford the rent. Others have been overpowered and outmaneuvered by their larger competitors. It seems like the only businesses left standing on that strip of West Broadway are global power brands and legacy Manhattan establishments that have been around for generations.

I've witnessed this war of attrition of small businesses in SoHo firsthand for the past several years.

Whenever another store is boarded up, I take a picture to remind me of how fortunate I am to survive another day in business. From time to time, I'll show the pictures to our staff to remind them what can happen to businesses if they take things for granted and if they don't constantly reinvent themselves.

It might sound paranoid or overdramatized, but the truth is that you have to earn the right to stay in business every day. Every day you make it in business is a blessing.

We've all been force-fed the same small-business survival statistics that intimidate every entrepreneur. Something like seven out of every 10 businesses fail in the first year, and nine out of every 10 fail in the first five years. But to see it firsthand as I do on my walk into the office every day and to read about it are two completely different sensations. The collateral damage behind each empty storefront is unknown but assumed. Behind each of them is a tale of job loss, depression, stymied creativity and negative impact to the local economy. I'm certain that these are the true stories behind each empty storefront.

When you're an entrepreneur, every day you stay in business is another day you get to play the game. The longer you play the game, the better your odds for beating the statistics and making something truly special happen over time.

My advice to entrepreneurs is to never get complacent, never take anything for granted and use little things like the SoHo streets to remind you of how much of a blessing it is to stay in business another day.

Who would've ever imagined that a short, four-block walk could serve as such a powerful lesson for me?

LESSON #17: SEIZE THE MOMENTS

One distinct difference I've noticed between being a twentysomething and a thirtysomething entrepreneur is the amount of game-changing opportunities that present themselves to you. The younger version of myself was lucky to get three or four opportunities each year with business-transforming potential, like global client prospects, talented new hires, breakthrough revenue generating opportunities and so on.

The older, more established version of myself is presented with these same opportunities on a much more frequent basis.

When I was right out of college, I remember reading a story about a young Ken Langone, who was an unknown banker in the 1960s when he was presented with the opportunity to represent Ross Perot as he took Electronic Data Systems public. Langone was persistent, saw an opportunity and seized it. He parlayed this opportunity into one of the most successful IPOs of all time, then started Home Depot, and the rest is history.

What is the moral of the story?

As a young entrepreneur, you need to *seize* these moments. Any one of them has the potential to change the trajectory of your business, so you can't allow them to pass you by. You don't know when the next one will come.

I was 27 years old and brand new to business when I was contacted by Acosta, a global, multibillion-dollar company in the consumer packaged goods (CPG) industry. Acosta was in immediate need of a media-training session for its newly appointed CEO. It searched far and wide for larger firms that were more established and had proven media-training programs in place. Fortunately for me, the larger competitors couldn't accommodate Acosta's quick turnaround project request fast enough.

Timing and circumstance led Acosta to put a call into me, an unproven twentysomething who was less than a year into starting a business. I had no media-training experience or formalized offering to speak of at the time. Despite this, Acosta, out of desperation, hired us on the spot.

Acosta paid me $10,000 for a three-hour media-training session, which was more money than any of our clients were paying us in an entire month at the time. The company flew me and my wife first-class to its headquarters in Florida, put us in an upscale hotel with a breathtaking ocean view and brought us to a five-star steakhouse the night before the training session. Not bad for a kid who, five years earlier, was scraping together quarters from between the couch cushions to buy a train ticket into Manhattan for my first job interview. I had never experienced anything like it before.

Truthfully, I had no business being awarded this engagement by Acosta, but nevertheless I found myself enroute to a blue-chip global company's headquarters with the opportunity of a lifetime.

Despite any insecurities or pressures that I felt because of the opportunity, I studied hard, prepared well and put on my bravest face. The end result was a very successful media-training session, and I left a good impression on Acosta's CEO and management team.

Acosta hired us as its full-time agency the next week. We converted the one-time training session into a recurring revenue opportunity that changed the trajectory of our entire business.

The engagement with Acosta became a multiyear relationship with a signature client that helped us to elevate our business to the next level and provided us with instant credibility during our formative years. It all began because I seized one of the very few game-changing moments that I was presented with back in the early days.

Seize the moments when they are in front of you. They will change your career.

LESSON #18: YOUTH *IS* A DIFFERENTIATOR

In the early days of our business, I remember making it to the final stage of many new business deals and client pitches only to lose them because of my age and inexperience. Many long and grueling pitch processes ended with a rejection email that looked something like this:

"Matt, we loved N6A and your energy, but we've decided to go with a firm that has been in business for a longer time and one that has a more experienced leadership team. It's nothing personal, but we felt like this was the best decision for our business at this stage."

While it was flattering that we made it to the final stage, the end result was a big, fat loss. Our income statement and our growth plans took no solace in knowing that we finished second to the competition. Where I come from, you don't get any points for being runner-up.

Fed up with finishing second, I decided that I wanted to learn from these losses. I began to think about how we could use our youth and inexperience to our advantage. Rather than go toe-to-toe with older, more established competitors and attempt to beat them at their own game, why not make age our differentiator and part of our unique selling proposition (USP)?

In these early days, I read several studies and reports that analyzed the most successful traits of entrepreneurs. The common threads of all the studies were traits such as persistence, creativity, self-belief, integrity, innovation and optimism.

What trait was missing from these studies? *Age* and experience. I quickly learned that there was no correlation between age and successful entrepreneurship.

There was no rule book that stated you had to be a certain age or in business for a certain amount of time in order to win.

From that point forward, we brought our youth into the pitch process early on and embraced our drive and vibrance as a differentiator. While we might not have had decades in business, we did have something that most of our larger, older competitors couldn't offer: energy, hunger and a burning desire to prove something. While our larger, older competitors lost this edge as they scaled, we had it in spades.

We took all the great qualities that our youth and energy had to offer and turned them into differentiators. "Embrace the Pace" became a mantra of ours and the centerpiece of our USP. We got the "Embrace the Pace" slogan trademarked. We tattooed it all over our marketing materials and merchandise for prospects to see. We leaned on qualities like speed, drive and scrappiness. These were things that we knew would play to our youthful and high-energy culture. Most importantly, we knew that these were things our larger, more established competitors didn't have. We turned youth into a *differentiator* rather than a *disadvantage*.

This was a pivotal turning point for our business. Prospective clients who previously passed on us suddenly told us that they appreciated our candor, our sense of purpose and the fact that we had something to prove. Rather than turn against us because we were young, we found that prospects began to hire us because they viewed our youth as an asset that would help them grow their businesses.

While we didn't close every deal, we did find that we were much more successful because we used our age to our advantage and made it part of our differentiators.

As you're navigating through your career and come up against older, more established competitors, think about how you can turn your youth and inexperience into an advantage. Chances are that with a little bit of resourcefulness and creative thinking, you can use this to your advantage.

Flip the script so that your youth is seen as a differentiator, not a disadvantage.

LESSON #19: BE A DATA DIVA

I used to think data was for geeks, but once I started operating a business, I quickly learned that it is one of the most valuable tools you can use in order to do your job better. In fact, it is an essential tool that you need at your disposal. You can't manage properly without having data in front of you.

This doesn't just apply to business operators and CEOs. No matter what role you're in or what your experience level might be, you should develop an ongoing rigor and process to analyze data as it relates to your department or function. This will help you understand performance trends and make incremental progress that will ultimately maximize your performance over time.

Over the years, I've become quite the data diva. I like to see everything presented to me in analytics.

When it comes to sales trends, I like to see data cut by industry, account value, pipeline growth, referral sources, deal cycle timeline, close rates by month and conversion rate on our paid media expenditure.

When I look at client retention patterns, I prefer to analyze the data by vertical, account manager, contract duration, customer satisfaction ratings and quarterly attrition trends.

When it comes to employee retention, I like to analyze who we lost by level, by reason, to whom and in which market.

In the recruiting function, I study candidate close rates by job title, resume type, salary range and the average duration of the offer process.

When it comes to IT, I prefer to sit down and study software expenditure by department, capacity usage, comparisons to prior years and the relationship of software upgrades to revenue performance.

You get the point.

Data is an incredibly valuable tool to help you maximize your performance no matter what role you're in. Data also enables you to A/B test things in your job.

Take the recruiting process, for example. Let's pretend we have Candidate A and Candidate B applying for two different positions at our company, and we want them *both*. Candidate A is a senior candidate applying for a leadership position and Candidate B is a junior candidate applying for an entry-level position.

They each go through the same process: a screening call, an in-person interview, reference checks, a thorough review of 401(k) and healthcare benefits, a review of quality of life and company perks, and finally extending an offer.

Candidate A accepts the job while Candidate B declines. Why did that happen?

It turns out that Candidate A had a family and was most interested in 401(k) and healthcare benefits, while all that was on Candidate B's mind was "How much am I going to get paid, how cool are the perks, and how much time off do I get?"

Next time around, when Candidate B is in the office, we would probably rethink the sequencing. Perhaps we would go right into perks, quality of life and growth opportunities for this candidate, burying the 401(k) and healthcare piece until later in the process. Then we would study the close rates to see if Candidate B would convert to an accepted offer after we made the adjustment.

The bottom line is, without the data and analytics at your disposal, you would never be able to diagnose and fix this issue for the future. The same is true of any department or role in which you're operating. I've yet to find a function, department or position within our company that can't be improved through smart and disciplined data and analytics.

If you really want to get ahead in your career, be a data diva!

However, don't forget that data is simply a tool. Turn to the next lesson for a word of caution when it comes to data.

LESSON #20: DATA WITHOUT DISCRETION IS DESTRUCTION

So, data is a valuable tool. But never forget, it's just a *tool*. Data is there to inform you, to educate you and to help guide you on the decisions that you make, but it should never make the decisions for you.

Data without discretion is *destruction*.

Ultimately, your brain should always be the judge and jury on your decisions.

I've always found that your ability to use discretion is where the rubber meets the road when it comes to decision making. Some of the most damaging mistakes that I've made as a manager have come when I was over reliant on data and under reliant on my discretion.

In the summer of 2017, we went through a string of unusually devastating new business losses. We usually closed qualified prospects at a 60 percent rate, but during this particular summer we barely closed anything. I think our close rate was under 20 percent during that summer.

Prospects that we would normally close in our sleep were rejecting us in favor of signing with competitors that we used to run circles around. It was a painful and frustrating time.

I studied the data inside and out to come up with a diagnosis. There had to be something wrong with our pricing, right? Maybe there was a problem with the pitch teams we deployed. Perhaps there was a breakdown during one of the stages of the pitch process. Maybe the sales deliverables weren't up to speed. Clearly, the solution had to lie somewhere in the data, right?

I was *dead* wrong.

That reality was that *I* was the problem.

I was really off my game that summer and it was severely impacting our sales performance. We had a lot of stuff going on. We were juggling a major move to our new headquarters in New York, and the $500,000 price tag for the annual rent was keeping me up at night. We were opening a new office in Toronto and relocating some employees from our New York operation. We were about to put ink on paper on our first acquisition of another company. Additionally, we were hiring new employees faster than we could keep up with. Things were absolutely insane that summer.

My head wasn't in the right place and I wasn't my normal self when it came to interacting with sales prospects. I was unusually short-tempered, unflattering and didn't spend the time that I normally would studying and preparing for prospect pitches. I showed up totally unprepared for meetings, I didn't have the right temperament and I was impatient. I wasn't in the right headspace to be an effective salesman during that time.

One prospect even told me that they would rather work with a college public relations intern than me. That one really hurt.

That is why we were losing the deals, not because of anything I saw in the data. Truth is, I knew I was the problem in my gut. But instead of doing something about it with my brain, I over-studied the data. Consequently, I ended up making some pretty serious changes to our pricing model, our sales processes and our approach.

If I had just exercised better discretion and been less dependent on the data, I would have let the crazy moves of that summer pass and then got back to closing business at our typical rates once fall came. But I didn't do that, and the subsequent changes I made were pretty severe.

We ended up overspending to fix problems that never existed in the first place. We made some stupid adjustments to our pricing that ended up diluting our offering. We put new processes in place that were redundant, unnecessary and costly. We scrapped our old sales materials, which were perfectly satisfactory, in favor of new ones that were overly complicated, long and non-user friendly.

This is just one example of analysis by paralysis, but I could give countless others. Whenever I've used data as a *tool* but discretion as the judge, it has led me to good places in my decision making. However, whenever I've used data as both a tool *and* the judge, it's been a disastrous combination.

Don't forget, you have a brain for a reason. Data without discretion is *destruction*.

LESSON #21: IMPACT IS THE MOST VALUABLE CURRENCY

At age 33, I realized that my greatest moments of pride came not necessarily in the most profitable of months, but in seeing the growth and emergence of others around me.

When I was in my late 20s into my early 30s, I placed a disproportionate value on money over impact (more on this in "Lesson #80: The Meaning of Money"). It's easy for me to say this now, but back then, with a wife at home and three children to support, I felt a lot of pressure to provide income for my family. I always thought that the more money I would make, the happier I would be in the office. Of course, money is important, and running a business for a profit is an absolute must when you're a bootstrapped entrepreneur with a family at home.

However, in time I found that I was happiest at work not necessarily when I made the most money, but when I saw the achievements of others around me. This became one of the most important lessons that I learned as a business leader.

Impact is the most valuable currency in which a leader can transact.

The lightbulb moment for me happened sometime around 2016. By that point, we had achieved sustained financial success by most small business standards. We had not only survived a half decade in business, but the company was consistently bringing in over $1 million in profit year after year. However, deep down inside I felt shallow and unfulfilled in the workplace during many of those years, despite having positive cash returns. Even though I was making money during that time, I hadn't yet found true partners and an inner circle with which I felt the company could grow.

That all changed as we scaled over the years. By 2016, I started to hire great talent that I truly believed in. These were people with whom I saw a future. They were people in whom I wanted to invest, and people I wanted to join me on my own career journey.

Many of these people grew within the company, moved into positions of leadership and contributed to our growth. Some stayed and became part of my inner circle, rising to our C-suite. Some left and moved onto greener pastures and accomplished great things at other places, being headhunted for the most important jobs in our industry.

In some way, all of them made their own contributions and left an indelible mark on our company's growth and history. To my surprise, seeing these bets that I made on people pay off gave me more happiness than any of our most profitable quarters or years.

Knowing that in some small way I had impacted them and their career trajectory was very meaningful to me. I found it to be infinitely more meaningful than any cash return we had ever seen. I never realized how much gratification the impact on others would bring to me until this happened.

To this day, I still run our business with a keen eye toward profitability. When you're the sole shareholder of a business, you're the one who's taking all the financial risk. Naturally, there is a commensurate return that you should expect for taking that risk. However, you should never confuse that with happiness.

In time I've learned that the most valuable currency you can transact in as a business leader is impact. It will bring happiness and fulfillment unlike any other currency can. It puts cash to shame.

LESSON #22: THE "DO SOMETHING DIFFERENT" RULE

Every year you should do something that *nobody* else in your industry is doing. I started doing this back in our first year of business. Over a decade later, it remains a keystone to my growth and progress as a professional.

The first time I tried this out, in 2010, almost everyone in our industry was doing billable hours and filling out time sheets, so I figured we might as well try something different. I spent a considerable amount of time developing a new model that was the antithesis of billable hours. We created a model that was based on key performance indicators (KPIs) instead of time. Ten years and millions of dollars later, this model is still working out well for us.

In 2013, my youngest daughter, Simona, was born. The morning after she was born, I woke up and took a stroll to the bookstore before I reunited with my wife at the hospital. In the store, I read about an all-expense-paid trip to Hawaii with which Salesforce.com rewarded its top sales performers. I took that concept and ran with it. A few weeks later, I came up with something we called the "N6-get-Away" and "Bucket List" competitions to reward our top performers. Seven years and many trips to the Amalfi Coast, Bali, Paris, Santorini and Sundance Film Festival later, these competitions remain inextricably connected to our brand. They are among the things we're best known for in our industry. They are a constant topic of interest and differentiation in every conversation we have with potential candidates.

In 2016, I remember listening to a podcast with JP Morgan Chase CEO Jamie Dimon. He was discussing a new cross-country bus tour initiative the firm had just rolled out. The bus tour was a way for the company's executives to solicit honest and open feedback from employees across the United States.

"Everyone gets a beer and immunity," he said on the interview, as a way of encouraging brutally honest feedback from employees without consequences.

From that point forward, we created a monthly "Coffee and Immunity" series. During these sessions, I sit in the conference room and answer any and all questions on the minds of our employees. Questions are answered in a fully transparent and confidential setting. The only rule is that you can't badmouth a co-worker. Everything else is on the table and fair game. Our "Coffee and Immunity" series has become an important initiative for us. It has been well received by our employees and has led to my receiving much-needed feedback to help improve our company in many ways.

In 2017, I remember walking into one of my favorite grocery stores. Once I had finished shopping, a customer service representative approached me with an iPad, asking me to rank my experience in the store from one to 10. As soon as I was handed the iPad, I thought to myself, "Wouldn't it be cool if we developed our own customer ranking system, so our clients could rank us every month?"

Out of this experience, our Customer Power Ranking System was born. It remains one of our greatest examples of innovation as a company to this day. Each month, our clients receive text-enabled messages that provide them with an opportunity to rank their service experience with us.
This initiative has helped us align with our clients and receive constant checkpoints in order to assess their level of satisfaction.

No matter where you're at on your career journey, I would encourage you to do something every year that nobody else in your industry is doing. It can be as simple as adopting a new way of servicing your customers or as elaborate as some of the examples I have shared here.

Doing something different will create uniqueness from your peer set. It will also serve as a vehicle for you to constantly progress, improve and innovate in your career.

Be *different*. It's a good thing.

LESSON #23: FALL IN LOVE WITH THE PROCESS

Just before I started our company, my mother gave me a framed card with a saying on it. It still hangs in my office today and has become one of my favorite quotes:

The process is the most important part of the journey. Appreciate it while you have it.

Just like building a successful career, there is a process and an arc that comes with building a successful business. The hardest part is that so much of the process and arc is unpredictable (see "Lesson #40: Enjoy the Curves"). The process is every type of emotion you can imagine. It's stressful, rewarding, tiresome, gratifying and everything else you can think of.

Here's the one thing I've learned over the years.

Fall in love with the *process*, not the outcome.

You absolutely have to fall in love with the process of building your career or business. It's actually a beautiful thing if you can discipline yourself enough to make time to enjoy it. You don't always see it in the moment, but as you're building your career or business, you're going through a brand-new process at every stage.

There's the "survival" stage at the beginning (see "Lesson #1: Never Forget the Survival Days"). There's the "evolution" stage, when you're moving into growth mode. There's the "adjusting" stage, when you have to pivot. There's the "eulogy" stage, when all is said and done (see "Lesson #42: Eulogy Over Resume").

It's easy to lose sight of the beauty and purpose of the process when you're dealing with the emotions at each stage, but you need to enjoy it. I find that when I look back at things, I tend to smile and enjoy them more than I did in the moment. Many of my regrets come from not stepping back and enjoying the process as I was going through it.

All of this has happened because I've been consumed by chaos in the heat of the moment. But the truth is, there is always going to be chaos, and if you don't step back and enjoy it then you're going to let important memories in your career slip away.

The process is what makes the journey fun. It's the chase that is addicting, not the finish line. All the moments that you go through during the process build your professional character and identity. Even though you don't see it in the moment, when you're going through the process you're learning, improving and reinventing yourself. Now that's the fun stuff.

Nowadays, I make a concerted effort to a better job of enjoying the process. Whenever I go through the inevitable curves of running a business — revenue ebbs and flows, painful mistakes, management mishaps, challenges with people and wrong decisions — I try to remind myself that it's all part of the process. As I've progressed through my career, I've learned to enjoy and appreciate the process much more than I did in my younger years.

Take it from someone who has been too focused on the finish line. It's the chase that's fun.

Slow down and *enjoy* the process.

LESSON #24: GIVE A GLIMPSE, NOT A TOUR

One lesson I've found has served me well over the years is to humanize the experience between your company and your customer.

What does this mean exactly?

If you're running a company, bring customers into your world internally. Give them a glimpse of what it's like to work at the company, what makes it special, what your operating principles are, and how you run your processes. Customers will appreciate this level of transparency and view it as a point of differentiation between your company and other service providers with which they are engaged.

The same thing goes for your employees — give them a glimpse into how your customers run their operations, what it's like to work there, and the unique stories they have to offer. Employees will appreciate this, as it will give them exposure to new types of businesses and broaden their horizons. Also, if you're running a good business, it should give them a newfound appreciation for working at your company and demonstrate that the grass isn't always greener on the other side.

Doing this will humanize the relationship between your team and your customer. It creates a much more human experience and synergy between the two teams, which will serve the relationship well, particularly in the most challenging of moments. When those challenging moments inevitably come, you will know more about your customer than most outsiders since you've taken a peek behind the curtain already. Likewise, your customers will understand your DNA in those moments since they've gotten a glimpse of how things are run.

There is an important distinction and disclaimer, though.

Give them a *glimpse*, not a *tour*.

You should give the customer enough to see how your operation is run and to demonstrate that you're doing something right. But don't let them sniff around too much. It never ends well when you do that. It's a fine line, and you must walk it carefully. Just give them enough to appreciate you, but don't overload them with too much inside information so they can start scrutinizing things to your detriment.

One time I remember a prospective customer was interested in our performance rewards program and was adamant that they understand how we incentivize our employees before they signed with us. We had developed a unique performance rewards program called Pace Points that had received acclaim, and the prospective customer wanted to understand it before they hired us as their service provider. I went against my better judgment and agreed to give the prospective customer a full-blown demo of the rewards system. I showed them everything about the program, including how it was modeled, how employees could redeem their points, and how we handled accounting and logistics for the program.

This turned out to be a horrific mistake, as the prospective customer was merely on a fishing expedition and had no interest in hiring us as their service provider. They just wanted free intelligence to help them model their own employee rewards program. I committed a cardinal sin, and agreed to give the customer a tour, not just a glimpse. That was a painful lesson and one that I will never make again.

Remember, when it comes to your relationships with customers, glimpses are good. Tours are terrible.

LESSON #25: PROMISE, DELIVER

If I had a dollar for every time I heard someone espouse the virtue of underpromising and overdelivering, I would be well into my retirement on the Adriatic Coast by now.

I've always found the notion of underpromising and overdelivering to be inherently dishonest, despite what most people would lead you to believe. It's certainly just as dishonest as the notion of overpromising and underdelivering, as I see it.

Anytime I've ever overpromised something to a customer — in other words, whenever I've made a promise that I know would be hard to live up to — it has been a guaranteed recipe for failure. I'm sure this doesn't come as a surprise to you. You should never overpromise. I've learned this lesson the hard way, particularly in the earlier days of my career journey.

Just like me, you've probably been trained to underpromise and overdeliver. Well, I'm here to tell you that that concept is just as flawed and dishonest as overpromising and underdelivering.

Anytime I've ever underpromised something to a customer — in other words, whenever I've made a promise that I knew would be so easy to deliver that it was far below our standards — it has also been a guaranteed recipe for failure. In those situations, I have felt like I wasn't being true to myself and that I was selling short my capabilities and my fiduciary responsibility to the customer, which is to optimize my performance on its behalf. The end result has typically been the same as in the scenario where I overpromised. It never ends well.

So, here's a novel concept that very few preach but that all should wear on their sleeve like a badge of honor.

Promise. Deliver. Rinse. Repeat.

You should tell a customer what you *believe* you can deliver. Nothing more, nothing less. Then step up and *deliver* what you said you would, and do it over and over again. Honesty, transparency and self-confidence. Now that's what it's all about!

Think about all of the times you've been in a car dealership with an unctuous salesman who is making promises you know he can't live up to. "Well, Johnny, I have no doubt that I can get you in this car for your budget!" the salesman says.

Right…

Meanwhile, you haven't even disclosed your budget to him yet, so how could he possibly know what it is? You just know that's BS. He's clearly *overpromising*.

Now think about being in the car dealership with the same salesman, except he completely underpromises instead of overpromising. "Well, Johnny, it's going to be very tough for me to get you in this car for your budget," the salesman says.

Meanwhile, he's just telling you that to manage your expectations and set you up to be pleasantly surprised when he gets you closed for a price that you believe was a bargain but that, in reality, was far from it.

Both approaches are a major turnoff in my mind. I'd rather the salesman just be forthright with me and tell me what he believes he can deliver, and see if it's a match for my needs.

The same rule should apply to sales, service, and any other aspect of your dealings with customers and peers in the workplace.

Don't overpromise. Don't underpromise.

Promise. Deliver. Rinse. Repeat.

Now that is a winning formula right there.

LESSON #26: LISTEN TO SMARTER PEOPLE, MAKE YOUR OWN DECISIONS

My father was smarter than me when I sat with him at his kitchen table in the winter of 2009, and he is still smarter than me today.

My father had a very successful career, but always made sure his job took a backseat to his family. He never missed a family dinner, a Little League game or a school play. Consequently, I always felt that he never reached the earnings or had the financial trappings of success that he could have achieved. I've always done the best job I could when it comes to my family life, but the truth is it's impossible to be an entrepreneur without it impacting your home life in some way. I've always admired this about my father. He's always had a well calibrated moral compass and set a great example for me as a role model.

But make no mistake. My father is one of many people who I count as much smarter than me, and someone to whom I've always gone for career advice.

So, there I sat with him at the kitchen table in his house in the winter of 2009, about to ask for his advice on this start-up business idea I had called North 6th Agency. I was 26 years old, had recently surpassed the $100,000 income threshold at my job, and was rising pretty quickly through the ranks of my profession.

When I showed him my business plan and asked for his advice, he looked at me and told me that I was crazy.

"Now is not the right time," he said like a true father. He began listing all the reasons why he felt I would be taking unnecessary risk by starting the business at that time.

"You have a steady income, you have a pregnant wife to support, and there is an economic crisis," he said. He had some valid points.

I listened. I digested. I internalized. Then *I decided*.

Fast-forward a few months later. I found myself in a lawyer's office signing the articles of incorporation for my business, and a few months after that we officially opened our doors.

I knew in my heart that I wouldn't be able to live with myself if I didn't give it a shot. So, I went for it. And I went all in, despite my father's advice.

The rest is history. My father has been there at every step of the way with me as I've built our business. Even though he didn't agree with the decision when I first made it, he ultimately got behind me, and did everything he could to support me once I made my decision. That alone is an important lesson about parenting. Even though my father didn't agree with my decision, he supported it and from that point forward he decided he would do everything he could to make sure the decision worked out for me. My father has been a great sounding board for me ever since, and has been there for me through my darkest moments in business.

What's the main lesson of this story?

I've learned that you should always listen to people who are smarter than you, but ultimately you are in the driver's seat. You are the only one who can make the tough decisions when it comes to your career.

The story of my father's advice is just one of hundreds of examples I could share with you. Through the years, I've been fortunate enough to build a great network of people who are smarter, more intuitive and more pragmatic than I am. I've always listened to them, and most of the time I've done as they have advised. But I've found that the most successful decisions that I've made in my career have actually come when I went *against* the advice of smarter people.

My father is still smarter than me today, but even he would agree that I made the right decision at that kitchen table in the winter of 2009.

LESSON #27: LET THE COMPETITION FUEL YOU

My perspective on competition has evolved quite a bit in the decade since I first heard a speech by Amazon founder and CEO Jeff Bezos. When I was just starting our business, I heard Bezos give a speech about being customer-obsessed versus competitor-obsessed.

Bezos argued that, while most businesses claim to be customer-obsessed, they were actually competitor-obsessed. To this day, I couldn't agree more with this statement. If I had to guess, 98 percent of companies are obsessed with the competition even though they claim to be obsessed with the customer. But what it took me years to realize was that *obsessing* over the customer and *studying* the competition are not mutually exclusive.

If given the choice, I would always err on the side of obsessing over the customer instead of the competitor. This principle has guided me for most of my business career. However, in my youth and naivety, what I missed in Bezos' speech was that, by being customer-obsessed, it doesn't mean you can't let the competition fuel you. I had interpreted Bezos' ideology as a free pass to disregard everything and anything the competition was doing, when in reality I should have been *studying* the competition but *obsessing* over the customer.

When I was younger, I was completely disinterested in the competition. I viewed the competition as nothing but noise, clutter and an unwelcomed distraction from running my business. All I wanted to do was obsess over the customer. In some warped and twisted way, I thought that the competition would somehow force me to compromise our originality and innovation as a business, and it would trickle down to the customer service experience being impacted in a negative way. I was completely devoid of any ability to see the competition as a link to helping me get better.

That was a completely immature and insecure way of viewing the competition.

The truth is, the competition should *fuel* you.

Your competitors should make you hungrier, stronger and better. They should drive you to fight harder every day and to earn the right to stay in business.

In time, I learned to become a much more astute and studious CEO when it comes to the competitive landscape, while still maintaining a healthy obsession over the customer.

If we lose business nowadays, I want to know which competitor beat us and why. If we lose out on a blue-chip candidate, I want to know which competitor he or she chose to work for and why. If there's something we're not doing a good job of, I want to know which competitors are doing a better job of it and why.

Becoming a more disciplined student of the competitive landscape has helped me elevate my game as a CEO. It's enabled me to maintain the same level of hunger and desire to win as ever before, while keeping me humble and teaching me there is always room for improvement. No matter how great you are, there's always something that a competitor is doing a better job of than you. And no, by letting the competition fuel you, it doesn't mean that you're not obsessing over the customer.

LESSON #28: WE ARE ALL UNPROVEN AT THE NEXT LEVEL

In 2011, I was putting the finishing touches on our inaugural year in business. I was introduced to an older, well-respected gentleman who ran a successful consulting firm that had scaled considerably since he founded the business. I was looking for some advice on how to scale to the "next level" and he was kind enough to take me out to dinner.

He said that out of 100 entrepreneurs who tried to do what I did in their first year, maybe 20 of them would have succeeded. "Congratulations, you are one of 20," he said. I immediately asked him what it would take to get to the "next level," and he said that of those 20 entrepreneurs, only about 10 would get there.

He offered me advice on what it would take to be successful at the "next level" — hiring, infrastructure, delegation and cost structure — things that weren't even a blip on my radar that would suddenly become a necessity to scale to the "one of 10" stage. I spent the next year listening to his advice, and our company became "one of 10."

The following year, he told me what it would take to get to the "one of five" stage — innovation, risk assessment, financial discipline and P&L management.

More than a decade later, we still meet for dinner each year and discuss surpassing each stage and what it will take to scale to the "next level."

The one common thread is, there always seems to be a "next level," no matter how good you are at your job, no matter how big your business is, and no matter what your aspirations might be.

My ultimate career goal is to one day build N6A into a large, global company, and to run the organization alongside all the other people who helped get us there. The level of impact, stimulation and complexities that come with running a large company are the ultimate test for an executive. My goal is to one day put my management and leadership skills to the test at that level. Many people say founders and entrepreneurs are not effective CEOs of large companies, but I'm determined to defy that notion. I am motivated by the challenge of proving myself at the next level.

To this day, I still hear doubters and naysayers tell me, "Matt, you are a great entrepreneur, but you are unproven at the next level." This drives me to keep getting better and working on my skills so that one day I can successfully manage a business of that scale. I've spent a lot of time thinking about this over the years, and here's the lesson that I've learned.

We are all unproven at the "next level."

If you're a first-time manager, guess what? You are unproven at the "next level."

If, after spending the past several years in different mid-level financial management roles you've recently been promoted to Chief Financial Officer, guess what? You're unproven at the "next level."

If you're an office administrator who now has responsibility for handling inventory for a second office, guess what? You're unproven at the "next level."

If you're the CEO of a publicly traded company who's dealing with an external crisis for the first time, guess what? You're unproven at the "next level."

The truth is, there's always a "next level," and it means different things to each of us. No matter who you are and what you're looking to accomplish in your career, you will always have a "next level" at which you're unproven.

Being unproven at the "next level" has become a great source of motivation for me. I hope there is always a "next level" for me, and I always get the chance to prove that I belong there, just like I hope you can prove that you belong at the "next level," too.

LESSON #29: MAKE SOMEONE PROUD, PROVE SOMEONE WRONG

There are two questions that I ask all candidates when I interview them:

"Can you tell me the name of someone you want to make proud?"

"Can you tell me the name of someone you want to prove wrong?"

I feel these are the two most powerful things that you can learn about someone on your team. We all have someone in our lives we want to make proud, and we *certainly* have someone who doubted us at some point who we want to prove wrong. In some way, our work serves as a stage for us to perform so that we can make these people proud and prove them wrong.

If you're wondering who mine are, here goes. I want to make my grandparents proud, and I want to prove all the doubters in "Lesson #41" wrong.

As soon as I ask candidates for the names of each person, I feel that I am now invested in their journey to make that person proud and prove the other person wrong. From that point forward, we're united in our quest to make someone proud and to prove someone wrong.

Employees over the years have told me some incredible stories about people they want to make proud and the ones they want to prove wrong. The "make proud" list has included everyone from deceased parents and loved ones to disabled family members and people whose couches our employees slept on as they were trying to survive in New York City.

The "prove wrong" list has included everyone from former co-workers who backstabbed our employees to ex-boyfriends, girlfriends and spouses, and high school teachers who told our employees that they didn't have the chops to cut it in college.

When it comes to my team, I can tell you each of the names of the people my direct reports want to make proud and the ones they want to prove wrong. I can probably tell you the "make proud" and "prove wrong" names of close to half of our entire employee base. Not bad, right?

One of my New Year's resolutions in 2020 was to learn the names of the people *everyone* in the company wants to make proud and the ones they want to prove wrong. I'm aiming for a 100 percent accuracy rate. This is important to me, and if you're a manager of people, it should be important to you, too.

Over the years, I've saved every thank you card anyone has written me and I added them to the wall in my office. It has grown to a collection of a few thousand cards and notes by this point, all of them from a variety of past and present employees, former and current clients, work friends and industry peers who I have met along the journey. This is my "bet on" wall. These are the people who have bet on me over the years, and clearly belong as an extension to the list of people I want to make proud.

On the other side of my office, I have saved a handful of notes and a list of names of people who didn't believe in me. This is my "bet against" wall. These are the people who doubted me over the years and clearly belong as an extension of the list of people I want to prove wrong. I'm proud to say this is a list that doesn't include many names, but it exists nonetheless, and it drives me to get the most of out of myself in the office each day.

Every day of your career should be a mission for you to make someone proud and to prove someone wrong. You should also be just as invested in your people's mission to do the same.

Next time you go into the office, put these two names on your wall, and ask your closest co-workers to give you their "make proud" and "prove wrong" names. It will drive you to succeed and it will drive you to invest in your people's mission to succeed.

Make someone *proud*. Prove someone *wrong*. That is a *powerful* combination right there.

LESSON #30: THE ORG CHART ALIGNMENT TEST

As a CEO, sometimes I feel as if my life is consumed by org charts. How is the service team structured? How is the sales team organized? How is the support function set up? How would our organization look if we integrated with this company? Does this person have a dotted line or a direct line into this other person?

Lots of paper, lots of ink and lots of connecting lines. The structure of an org chart is all fine and dandy, but here's what really matters about the org chart.

How well aligned is your organization?

Over the years, I've developed something that I call an *org chart alignment test*. It has become an effective way for me to assess how strong our organization is structured and how well aligned everyone is on our company's goals.

Here's how the *org chart alignment test* works.

The first thing I do is remove myself from the org chart. Then I look at the next person at the top of our organization. Usually, this would be our Chief Operating Officer or our President. Then I proceed to draw a circle around their name and their spot on the org chart.

Once I complete this exercise, the next thing I do is look all the way down to the bottom of the org chart and locate the most junior employee in the company. Typically, this would be an entry-level employee who just joined our firm, an administrative assistant, or a college intern if it's the summer or winter season. Once I identify the most junior employee in the company, I then proceed to draw a circle around their name and spot on the org chart.

Then I ask myself the following question:

"Do I believe the person on the bottom of the org chart is equally as aligned on our company goals as the person on top?"

I've always felt that, if the most junior person in our organization was as well aligned as the most senior person, then we were doing something *right*. It might seem like a crazy concept, but time and time again it's proven to be spot on.

Great companies are made from synchronization, togetherness and full alignment from the top down in the organization. Therefore, I like to use the *org chart alignment test* as a litmus test to determine how well aligned we are from the top of the company, all the way on down to the bottom.

If we pass the *org chart alignment test,* I usually take a deep breath and smile. A passing test means that we've hired the right people lately and we're all destined to achieve common goals together. If we fail the *org chart alignment test*, I usually pull together all our managers to solicit their feedback and perspectives. On a failing test, we'll typically ask ourselves why there is a lack of alignment from the top down, where the disconnect is stemming from, what the cause is of the broken link and how we can we fix it.

If you're managing a team of people, I would encourage you to create a similar test. Look at the top of your team and the bottom of your team in terms of seniority. Ask yourself how well aligned you believe the two team members are on your common goals. If you ask the senior person and the junior person to recite the company's goals, will they tell you the same thing, chapter and verse, or will they be completely disconnected?

How well aligned is your team? Take the *org chart alignment test* and I'll bet you will learn a lot.

LESSON #31: RESULTS ARE THE GREAT EQUALIZER

Here's the cold, hard truth that I learned early on as a young entrepreneur. Ultimately, your results speak for themselves. It will take some time to build your reputation, and you'll likely make some mistakes along the way. However, you will get to a point quickly when you realize that your results will be the great *equalizer*.

Today, as a not-so-young entrepreneur (sigh!), I continuously pass this advice onto first-time entrepreneurs and young people who are just starting out in their careers. Like it or not, your results are going to cash your checks. You can't hide from results. They are what they are.

I remember when I was first starting out in my basement, with no access to capital, clients or connections. The playing field seemed like it was unfairly tipped in favor of my older and more established competitors. At least that's how I felt for the first few years in business. Rather than pout and cry about how unfair life was, I chose to embrace the benefits of capitalism, which is a system that rewards based on production and merit rather than age or experience levels.

As a young entrepreneur, I was flabbergasted by the number of companies that prioritized strategy over execution. *The Economist* published a report[1] finding that only 56 percent of businesses were successful in delivering results based on their strategic initiatives. *Harvard Business Review* published a similar study[2] finding that 67 percent of strategies fail because of poor execution.

Sure, strategy is important, but at the end of the day, isn't it all about results and execution when you're first starting out?

You simply cannot afford to squander opportunities in your early days when you're establishing a name for yourself. You need to build a track record of dependability and production early on.

Look at the greatest performers of our time. Audiences pay big money and have high regard for people like Madonna, Michael Jordan and Bradley Cooper at the box office and the ticket window. Why? Because they *produce* results each time that they perform their craft. You need to be seen in the same light by others. You should be seen as guaranteed money when it comes to delivering results. You need to be looked upon by others as a person that people want to bet on because they know you'll always deliver for them.

Ask yourself this question: Would you rather be a 55-year-old who doesn't deliver, or a 25-year-old who always delivers? It's an easy answer, and chances are your customers, managers and peers will feel the same way once you've shown them you know how to deliver. Don't forget, results don't discriminate against age, and you are ultimately in control of your results. As a young entrepreneur or career-minded professional, you should take results over strategy every day of the week.

I tell young professionals this all the time. Screw your age, screw your experience, screw your fancy degree. Show me your results. That's what you want to be judged on.

Results are the great equalizer. Don't be scared. Just produce.

LESSON #32: INNOVATION IS BORN FROM EXPERIMENTATION

I have been surrounded by some incredibly innovative people throughout my career. Some of these people include brilliant product inventors, industry disruptors, visionary leaders and executives who have brought products to market before any of their competitors did.

Many clients and friends of mine have built technologies and patents that have been sold to the likes of Facebook, Google and Oracle. Several executives I know have created new and unique programs that have disrupted legacy functions such as accounting, healthcare, education and human resources. Beyond their contributions to the economy, many of them have made great contributions to society and humanity.

What's the one thing they have in common?

They love to *experiment*.

The most innovative people I've encountered in my career all treat their workplace as a test lab to create new ideas, tweak them, refine them and introduce them to the world.

I've found my own successes and failures in the area of innovation to be no different. All of my most innovative ideas, programs and points of differentiation were born from experimentation. As I look back at some of our company's greatest examples of innovation, all of them began with a simple experiment that we tested, refined, improved and then, years later, turned into something truly special.

In 2018, we saw an opportunity to disrupt the legacy public relations category with a service model that was geared toward business outcomes. The public relations industry had long been stuck in its ways, lacking any sparkle of innovation. For decades, the public relations industry had lagged behind its forward-thinking counterparts in the marketing services category, such as advertising and digital marketing, with antiquated practices and old-fashioned measurement methods that were no longer adequate for today's brands.

With this in mind, we decided to test out an experiment.

We began to develop a model of practicing public relations that tied to specific business outcomes. After many rounds through the test lab and several months of refinement, Outcome Relations was born. Today, it is the only example of a public relations service model that combines elements of earned media, paid media and measurement in order to drive a specific business outcome for a brand. We've taken this experiment all the way to the finish line, building out proprietary analytics and software, adding new pieces to our team, and creating trademarks and patents for the model.

Outcome Relations has become one of our greatest examples of innovation, and it has created clear and undisputable differentiation for our company against our competitive set.

It was all born from a simple idea that went through the test lab many times over, and came out the other end as a winner.

For every winning experiment, we've had 10 times the amount of losing ones.

Creating an overnight shift so that we could stay open for business 24/7? I've tried that one and it didn't have a happy ending.

Investing in a bitcoin team right before it crashed? Been there, done that.

Opening an office in San Francisco before I had ever stepped foot in the city? Yup, my head is still in my hands over that one.

These were all examples of losing experiments. There have been many more losing experiments over the years than winning ones. But the point is, you have to have the courage to try them in the first place. You need to know when to cut your losses on the ones that fail. The ones that hit will hit big, just like Outcome Relations did for us.

Experiment, experiment, experiment. In time, you will see that your greatest innovation is born from experimentation.

LESSON #33: DRINK PISS AND VINEGAR AND DO SOME CRAZY THINGS

Like many ambitious young professionals looking to make a name for themselves in their careers, I was full of piss and vinegar when I was in my 20s. I'm still every bit as ambitious as I was earlier in my career, though I'd like to think that I have matured a bit. The fluids I drink nowadays have become a much more refined and dignified version of piss and vinegar. Today, they're more like saliva and red wine. Or something like that. I'm sorry for the visuals, but I digress.

Chances are, if you're trying to accomplish something of significance at a younger age than most of your peers, you're going to have to do some crazy things to make yourself stand out. I did so many things that were crazy earlier in my career. Some of these crazy things hit big and some failed miserably, but I'm proud that I put myself out there and tried all of them. In many of the other chapters, I talk about the lessons learned from the ones that failed miserably, so for this lesson I want to focus on one that hit big.

When I was 28 years old, we were a finalist for a client account up against a firm that was much more established and proven than we were at that time. The CEO of the competing firm had about 20 years of life and work experience on me. The business was considerably larger, more established and well known than ours. It had a solid and stable clientele and a pristine reputation as a white-shoe public relations firm with offices all over the country. I knew that we wouldn't close the deal based on our merits alone, so I figured we would have to do something crazy to show greater effort and desire than our competitor in order to win the account.

The department to which we were pitching business was based in the United States, but the CEO of the prospective client was based in London.

As I thought about what we could do to stand out and win the account, I remembered a study[3] I had read which analyzed customer satisfaction and tip values for a group of waiters at various restaurants. The waiters who ended the meal experience proactively by offering mints and other personalized items for their customers got up to 21 percent better tips than the ones who didn't. If something as simple as adding mints could help with customer acquisition, imagine what doing something as crazy and personalized as a trip to another continent would do?

Before I knew it, I was on the first flight out to Heathrow. As soon as I landed several hours later, I made a beeline from the airport to the CEO's office. After convincing the front desk receptionist why she should let me in — which was a miraculous act in itself — I made my way into the CEO's office and greeted him with an assortment of gifts from New York. The package included bagels from Ess-a-Bagel, a platter of fresh meats from Katz's Deli, Yankees baseball merchandise and some other mementos from the Big Apple. Along with the gifts was a handwritten note from me and a verbal message telling him that we wanted to bring a little bit of New York swagger to London.

He was quite shocked and impressed by my commitment, so much that he put a call into the marketing department back in the United States to tell them about the gesture.

While the move was bold and time consuming, it helped us to win the account. More importantly, it taught me a valuable lesson. To stand out from your peer set, particularly as a young entrepreneur in a fiercely competitive environment, you're going to have to act boldly to overcome competitive challenges. Sometimes it's just a matter of showing that you want it more than anyone else and are willing to put your own personal touch on something to make it happen.

Drink piss and vinegar and do some crazy things. This is a good formula to stand out from the pack as you're making a name for yourself in your career.

LESSON #34: UNDERTRAINED AND OVERPREPARED

I am sure you've heard the phrase "fake it till you make it" at some point in your career. They should acid wash that phrase from business lexicon and ban it from being used for eternity. It is a terrible precedent to set, and in my experience, there is nothing that is further from the truth. You can't be successful by *faking* anything.

Although my job has evolved quite a bit since I first started our business, there are several functions that have remained core to my role since day one. Here are a few of them: *sales, management, customer service, operations, finance, recruiting, strategy.*

In some way, shape or form, these functions have intersected with my role at every stage of our company's growth.

I've never received one day of formal training in any of these areas. I've never been given a book on best practices on how to perform any of these functions, and if I did I probably wouldn't read it anyway. I've never had someone put their arm around me and say, "Kid, let me show you how to do this" for any of these tasks.

Somehow, I've managed to produce successful outcomes in each of these areas despite the fact that I have no experience or formal training in any of them.

Here's the key. You can be *undertrained* and *overprepared*.

I've found that any lack of formal training can be overcome with a tireless commitment to preparation.

In February 2010, I found myself pitching business to a Boston-based technology company named NetProspex. They were a fast-growing start-up in the data industry backed by some of the most prominent investors on the east coast. This was a big opportunity for me, as I desperately needed the revenue and the confidence boost to show me that I could close business on my own. The pitch was a multistage process that involved five other firms and myself, at the time a one-man operation working out of my basement with no paying clients and in business for less than one month.

The process included several steps, beginning with a request for proposal

(RFP), followed by an introductory call, then an in-person meeting to present ideas, plus a few other steps before the prospective client made a decision. I had never been through a simple sales process before, better yet something as elaborate as this.

I had never received an ounce of sales training, and honestly had no clue what the hell I was doing. For every step of the process I prepared tirelessly. I studied the company's business and its competitive landscape. I read about the company's executive team and which companies they'd previously worked for, which colleges they went to, and which hobbies they were interested in. I studied the company's capital structure, its investor bios and its job openings. To my pleasant surprise, the company kept inviting me back at every step, until eventually I got the call that I had been waiting for. Vice President of Marketing Mark Feldman informed me that I had won the account.

NetProspex became my first paying client, but more important than the retainer check was the lesson that I learned during this process. I saw firsthand that any lack of training I had could easily be overcome with tireless preparation. I was so proud when I won the account that I took my first check from them and hung it up in the study in my house. It was a small, prorated check of only a few hundred dollars, but that's beside the point.

The check hung on the wall for years until eventually the company's accounts payable team called, reminding me to cash the check or they would void it. I regret ever cashing that check. I should've let it hang there forever. It gave me so much joy and sense of accomplishment every time I saw it, and it reminded me of the value and importance of preparation.

To this day, I continue to bump up against people and companies who are much more qualified than I am based on their training and credentials. But I vow to never let anyone out-prepare me, and this has served me well in my career.

I would take overprepared over undertrained any day of the week. You can't "fake" anything.

LESSON #35: KEEP IT SIMPLE AS YOU SCALE

Scaling a business is difficult. Really difficult. This is especially true when it's your own capital, as I've learned in my experience trying to scale our business over the past decade.

When it's your own money, you have so much more to lose, and you're faced with capital restrictions that make scaling your vision to the next level a challenge. I've found that my blood pressure has increased and my hairline has receded commensurate with the size and scale of our operation. It comes with the territory, and I've learned to live with the stress at this point.

We are more than 10 times the size that we were after our first year in business, so we've scaled considerably over the years. However, I always felt we could be so much bigger and better right now if I just had done some things differently along the way.

Here's the most important lesson I've learned as we've scaled:

Keep it simple.

Scaling a business is difficult enough to begin with. You don't need to make it *more* difficult than it needs to be. I've had a tendency to feel the need to overcomplicate things in order to scale. In my own mind, I've told myself that scaling a business to the next level was so difficult that our own systems and processes needed to match that level of difficulty. That was dead wrong.

I've found that whenever I've added unnecessary layers of complexity to our company as we've scaled, it has inhibited our ability to grow. There have been years when I've implemented elaborate performance programs, infrastructure systems and incentive plans and identified acquisition targets and other strategic initiatives that were overly complicated and didn't align with our growth goals during those years. I observed that we got distracted anytime I did this. Our people were confused, and subsequently we grew nominally in those years, usually anywhere from five to 10 percent.

On the other hand, during years when I simplified our processes, making sure we had top-down alignment on company goals, making sure our departments were well synchronized and pulling in the same direction and our goals were communicated clearly and succinctly to our staff, we had our biggest growth years — usually 30 to 50 percent.

By keeping it simple, I mean simplicity in every sense. There should be simplicity in your processes, programs, communication methods, incentive structures and strategic initiatives you choose to pursue. The simpler and cleaner these initiatives are for everyone to understand, the better off you will be.

Even though we've scaled considerably, we still have a long way to go. I believe that we have a lot of room for growth, and one of my goals for the next 10 years is to transform N6A into a company with a global footprint. Our business is nowhere near the scale or size that I aspire for it be.

As we go forward, one commitment that I've made to myself is to avoid the trap of overcomplicating things. I'm just going to keep it simple.

If history has taught me anything, it's that we'll scale successfully if we follow this rule.

LESSON #36: OLD SCHOOL/NEW SCHOOL BALANCE

I have witnessed the workforce transform firsthand over the past decade. In our first few years in business, I was basically a big brother to many of our employees. In most cases, only a few years in age separated me from the employees I was managing, and the dynamic could best be described as fraternal.

I've always been very old-school in my approach to work, believing in principles such as discipline, hard work and accountability. As you can imagine, it was easy for someone like me to succeed in this type of management environment in the early days. I could give our younger employees tough love when I needed to and I didn't have to pull any punches. There was a disciplined foundation behind the way I managed that proved to be successful in our formative years.

Our younger employees responded well to this management style, mainly because they viewed me as a big brother and they came up through the same generation as I did. They preferred candor, professionalism and discipline in how they were being managed and were receptive to a process-driven approach. Over the years, this changed dramatically.

In time, millennials rose in power in the workplace and began to move from entry-level positions to management roles. As this was happening, I noticed a significant shift in the way our younger employees approached their work and what was important to them in their relationships with me as their boss. It was completely different from what had worked for younger employees in the earlier days.

While in the past younger employees preferred a much more *process-driven* approach to being managed, the millennials preferred an approach that was *purpose-driven*. There had to be a reason for every decision. Things needed to be explained and rationalized, and the younger employees needed to understand the relationship between the decision and the larger purpose. They wouldn't respond well to a task unless they understood how the task was connected to an outcome.

The old-school toughness and discipline that worked for me in our earlier years no longer resonated with the new generation that had risen in power in the workplace. The new generation demanded empathy, flexibility and compassion from me as a manager. The importance of the old-school virtues was clearly starting to diminish, and new-school traits such as these were becoming critical to forge successful bonds with those I was managing.

While it was difficult for me to adjust to this change in my management style at first, in time I found this to be one of the most gratifying learning lessons in my journey as a manager of people.

I couldn't stray too far from my old-school roots (it is who I am after all!), but I certainly needed to adapt to the new generation of the workforce if I was going to have any success as a manager going forward. With this in mind, I learned to balance the two and incorporate both into my management repertoire.

Old-school work ethic with *new-school empathy*.

I found this to be a very successful formula as I learned to manage the younger generation rising through the ranks. The younger generation saw that I was making a concerted effort to step outside my comfort zone, and these individuals appreciated that. They had an empathetic quality to them that I hadn't seen in my generation. However, they also liked that I brought a unique perspective and discipline with my old-school ways that would serve them well. There was a great balance of give and take that came out of our work relationships as a result. It was much more harmonious and less adversarial than I had anticipated. I learned a lot from them, they learned a lot from me, and working together we helped each other to achieve a great balance of old school and new school.

I'm sure a lot of this had to do with my age. Being in my early 30s at the time, I was at an ideal age to make this pivot. I wasn't too old to be stuck in my ways, but wasn't too young to lack perspective.

One of the proudest moments of my career was making this pivot. To this day, I get great enjoyment out of managing the younger generation. I find that I learn from them just as much as they learn from me. The old school/new school balance continues to serve me very well as a manager. I've also noticed that other managers in our company who are my age or older have been most successful when they've made the same adjustment, blending old-school qualities with new-school qualities in their management approach.

I'm interested to see what happens in the next decade, as the circle of work life continues to spin and the next generation rises to power. I'm sure the time will come when I have to make another major pivot to my management style in order to adjust to the new generation. Until then, I'm going to stick with the *old school/new school balance*. It seems to be working well.

LESSON #37: IN TIMES OF ADVERSITY, LEAN ON HUMILITY AND HUMOR

Throughout your career, your back is going to be against the wall many times. So much of your career will be defined by how you handle this adversity. I can think of many regrets in my career that came as a result of handling adversity poorly.

Panicking, thinking of myself before others, taking myself too seriously. These are examples of some of my failures in dealing with adversity.

In time, I've learned that humility and humor are the most effective qualities to lean on when you're faced with adversity.

In the spring of 2019, we had to close one of our offices in Canada. We did everything we could to make the office a success for years, but eventually we ran out of options. The office was burning a hole through our P&L and restricting us from making important decisions to invest in our core business. We had no choice but to shut it down.

This was a pretty devastating moment for me. As a result of poor decisions that I made as the leader of our company, we were forced to shut down an office, resulting in other people's jobs being eliminated, relocated or reduced. Several of them had been with our company for a long time. They were all exemplary employees and were nothing more than innocent victims of poor decisions that I made that led us to that point.

Anytime you're dealing with adversity like this, the most important thing to realize is that you are there to make *other* people's lives comfortable, not yourself. With the office being shut down, some people would lose their jobs while I got to return to New York the following day and resume my duties as CEO of the company.

Humility will guide you through adversity like this and help you get through it as best as possible. All of the aspects of humility — accepting responsibility, putting other people's interests before your own, helping others leave with dignity — proved to be an important lesson I learned during this time of adversity.

Similarly, I've found that having a sense of humor during times of adversity is also important.

Beyond the Canadian office closure, we've been faced with many other moments of adversity over the years. Just like any business, we've had to confront scary issues such as sales droughts, budget challenges, personnel problems and corporate crises. Just like humility is important,

I've found that leaning on your sense of humor will help you get through times of adversity.

Humor will help you keep things in perspective and remind you that everything will be all right. When you're in the midst of adversity, it seems like it's going to last forever and you're never going to make it out alive. In moments like these, your sense of humor will guide you through it just as your humility will. Your sense of humor will remind you that you'll get through everything, and you're not going to lose your career or business over it. And guess what? Your problems are probably insignificant compared to real problems in this world in the grand scheme of things.

Humility and humor. These are the best allies you can have when you're faced with adversity in your career.

LESSON #38: JUGGLE THE PAST, PRESENT AND FUTURE

One of the things that I enjoy most about being a CEO is that you have to juggle the past, the present and the future all at the same time to do your job successfully. I would imagine this to be true of any job or career path that you're pursuing.

Here's why each of the three is important.

You need to live in the *past* because that's where your greatest learnings will come from.

You need to live in the *present* because you have to focus on hitting results and executing in order to survive.

You need to live in the *future* because you have to have a vision of where you want to go, and a plan for how you're going to get there.

You see, all three are equally as important. I've found that anytime I've placed too much priority on one, something else has dropped as a result.

For example, whenever I've been overfocused on execution in the moment (i.e., the "present"), our competitors have beat me to the punch on a long-term strategy that we should have seen coming (i.e., the "future"). Whenever I've been overfocused on long-term strategy, I haven't been able to study our recent performance and get better as a result (i.e., the "past").

This is one of the most stimulating things about being a CEO. You know you need to focus on the past, the present and the future, but juggling those and managing your time accordingly are a big challenge.

For years I struggled to develop a system that would help me adequately juggle past, present and future. Then finally, in 2019, I decided to create a time map and share it with my direct reports. This map showed all of the parts of my job — culture, sales, finance, strategy and so on — and how much time I wanted to spend on each area in the new year. The words "PPF" were spelled out in bright letters on the time map.

Of course, "PPF" stands for "past, present, future."

I've learned to treat PPF as if it's a standard part of my job, just like any other function. Ten percent of my time each week goes to studying the past, 20 percent to executing on the present and 20 percent to strategizing for the future. The remaining 50 percent is dispersed across all the other areas of my job.

Since I first implemented the time map and allocated a chunk of my schedule to focus on PPF, I've become a more well-rounded executive. It's opened my eyes to new learnings from past mistakes, it's helped me stay disciplined about spending the necessary time to get ahead of long-term plans for the future, and it's also kept me pragmatic so that I never forget to execute in the present.

No matter what role you're in or where you're at on your career journey, I believe the PPF approach will help you become the best version of your professional self. Make time to learn from the past, execute in the present and strategize for the future.

The past, present and future. Once you figure out how to juggle them properly, the sky is the limit.

LESSON #39: BUILD AN IMPENETRABLE INNER CIRCLE

Let me tell you about the moment when I knew that I had built an impenetrable inner circle at work, and all of those long nights and early morning meetings had paid off.

In 2019, we were in discussions to be acquired by a private equity firm for a fee approaching $20 million and an additional investment of $100 million to scale our company through acquisitions and other investments. It would have literally been a dream come true for me in many ways. It would have provided me with a life-changing liquidity event for all of the hard work over the past 10 years, and more importantly, it would have given me the capital needed to scale our firm globally as I always dreamt of.

Just like with any investment or private equity deal, however, the harsh realities of post-acquisition life gave people on my team reason to be concerned. My team loved their lives at work and genuinely enjoyed the independence we had as a private, self-funded company, with no pressures from investors or board members. Even though we are disciplined, we've always had a great time in and out of the office, and we took full advantage of the freedoms that come with being independent.

A private equity deal would have changed everyone's lives as we knew it, some for the better, as was the case with me, and some potentially for the worse, as was the case with the others. The deal could have meant that we would be forced to make some tough decisions, including consolidation, implementing new board and governance structures, or even eliminating jobs. The truth is, I would've negotiated ironclad contracts for all of my people as a condition of the acquisition so their jobs couldn't be eliminated, but the thought of consolidation still freaked everyone out.

Many people in my inner circle, including my Chief Operating Officer and Chief of Staff, approached me.

"Matt," they said. "We know if we do this deal, we might lose our jobs."

I was silent, completely unable to process what was about to come next.

"But that's OK with us," they said. "You deserve this deal, and if it means we lose our jobs, we still want you to take it anyway."

In the end, the deal fell through, but I never forgot that display of selflessness. It was one of the most humbling feelings that I had ever experienced in my career. How could I possibly respond to something like that? It nearly brought me to tears.

It was at that very moment that I knew I had built an impenetrable inner circle. Who else would do that, knowing they could lose their jobs but still supporting the decision to take the deal because they wanted to see me have a successful outcome?

I realize how lucky I am to have the relationship that I share with my inner circle. They've shown me time and time again their commitment, selflessness and sacrifice for the greater good of the team.

I feel bad for anyone who doesn't have the same relationship that I have with my team, because I've seen firsthand how much more enjoyable, meaningful and exhilarating life in the workplace can be when you have an impenetrable inner circle — a group of people who will challenge you, inspire you, hold you accountable and ultimately support you, no matter how it might ultimately affect them.

It took me quite a while to build this rapport with my inner circle. It didn't just happen overnight. Just like any relationship, it took time, effort and constant compromises to build chemistry and develop an impenetrable bond with my team at work. There have been many late-night phone calls, weekend war-room sessions, impromptu road trips, and trying moments we have shared together. Even though you don't realize when it's happening, all of these moments are building a chemistry and bond that will pay off when you need it the most in your career, just like it did for me when we were in discussions with the private equity firm.

As disappointed as I was when we didn't get that private equity deal, it helped me appreciate that I had built something that very few in their career had — an impenetrable inner circle. In the end, I'm prouder of that than anything.

LESSON #40: ENJOY THE CURVES

I got knocked on my ass very quickly, and immediately learned that business is not a straight line. It's a curvy line with many unpredictable twists and turns along the way.

Here's the lesson I've learned.

Enjoy the curves.

One of the first times I understood that business was a curvy line was back in 2010 when I won a game-changing contract.

Al DiGuido awarded our company with a $300,000-per-year contract to service his account. Al was a longtime client and mentor, and someone for whom I had deep respect and admiration. He was a pioneer in the email marketing and publishing sector. He served as CEO of Bigfoot, Epsilon and Zeta Interactive, which was the company he was running when he awarded us the contract. As great of a businessman as Al was, he was an infinitely better man. He dedicated his time, money and energy to his lifelong passion of helping children with cancer and rare blood disease through his charity, Al's Angels.

Al could have awarded the contract to a larger firm, and I would have completely understood his decision. He had a lot riding on the decision as the CEO of a major global company. However, he was fiercely loyal and believed deeply in me, so he gave the contract to me instead of the larger suitors. I will never forget the trust and faith that Al placed in me for the rest of my life.

At 27 years old and less than a year into business, a $300,000 contract was like hitting the lottery. I thought that I died and went to heaven.

The euphoria was short-lived, however. A few months later, Zeta brought in a new CEO. It stopped paying its bills and ultimately sold off all its assets. I started to panic. The Zeta account represented nearly half of our revenue at the time. We had just signed a new lease on an office in TriBeCa, we had hired new employees and had put other expenses on our books, all under the assumption that we could count on the company's $300,000 contract.

I spent the next several weeks busting my ass to find revenue to replace Zeta's so that we could avoid making decisions that would disrupt our business, such as laying off employees or downsizing our office.

In the end, everything worked out for the best. We were able to replace Zeta's revenue rather quickly, and Al fought tooth and nail for us to recover some of the past dues that we were owed. He also introduced us to PM Digital, one of the companies that acquired Zeta. We entered into a relationship with PM Digital that lasted for many years.

Almost 10 years later, I was able to convince Al to come out of retirement and join us as we scaled our company to the next level. Today, I am proud to call him a teammate of mine and one of those I consider to be part of my impenetrable inner circle (remember "Lesson 39: Build an Impenetrable Inner Circle"?).

Talk about a wild curve ball! This curve ball has lasted for 10 years. It has taken me from the highs of the high (a $300,000 annual contract) to the lows of the low (a near-fatal blow to my business) and then back to the highs of the high again (a new client, and a reunion with Al as we build our company to the next level).

What's the moral of this lesson? Your career is not a straight line. It's a curvy line that will take you to unpredictable places and will hit you with surprises when you're least expecting them. Even though it can be difficult, try to enjoy the curves when they come. The curves constantly keep you on your toes and usually take you to better places if you're able to absorb them when they hit you.

Forget about the straight lines. Enjoy the *curvy* ones.

The *curves* are what make your career fun.

LESSON #41: HOW TO DESTROY THE DOUBTERS

I have never forgotten anyone who has doubted me in my career. In fact, I owe just as much of my success to the doubters as the believers. Their doubt of me has driven me to improve, self-reflect and get better as a professional.

We all encounter our fair share of doubters over the course of our careers. I am certainly no exception to this. I've had countless people through the years tell me that I couldn't do something. They told me I wasn't intelligent enough, I wasn't experienced enough, I didn't have the right pedigree, I didn't have the right temperament.

While the negative energy from the doubters can be kryptonite to your career, I've found that the doubters have actually contributed to my progress and success. Over time, I've learned to destroy the doubters through constant *innovation*, *work ethic* and *self-reflection*.

In 2016, I started to see the need for better technology and performance analytics in our industry. I found that public relations firms weren't doing an adequate job of measuring internal performance and setting goals for their employees. No agencies of our size had a tool to accurately measure the performance of their employees and to align their performance with the key performance indicators (KPIs) of clients.

I spent several months drawing up a blueprint for a software tool that would address this need and how we were going to raise money to fund its development and commercialization. After all, we were a small, self-funded start-up at the time, and in order to do this right I would need to raise capital.

I hit the road and lined up a handful of meetings with venture capitalists from my network out in San Francisco. One of the meetings I was able to secure was with a well-known venture capitalist who had invested in several data and analytics companies. He had a reputation of being a hard-ass, as I quickly found out.

I sat down with him and pitched him on my vision to build analytics software that would create alignment between employee performance and customer expectations. It was going to be a three-year development and commercialization process. We were going to spend the first year developing the tool, then the following year beta testing it on our own employees, and then the next year we would monetize it by selling it to other service providers in the public relations industry.

The meeting wasn't even 10 minutes in when the venture capitalist said to me this idea was dead on arrival.

"You're not a freaking technology company — you would never get a dime from me," he said. "You're nothing more than a services company. I hate when people like you *pretend* to be someone you're not."

"People like *you*!?" I thought. It wasn't so much *what* he said but *how* he said it that got my blood boiling. He was patronizing, pretentious and arrogant.

The meeting was over right there. He clearly doubted me. He doubted my vision and my ability to add an innovative technology component to a legacy services business such as public relations. I saw the vision as filling a void in a legacy industry, while he saw it as someone who was trying to build something that they weren't capable of building.

I spent the next several months in constant self-reflection, thinking about that meeting, intent on making him eat his words.

Eventually, we ended up self-funding the project. It wasn't easy to set aside the capital in our budget, but in the end I'm glad we did it.

After a few years of behind-the-scenes modeling, we finally brought on an in-house software developer in 2018 to get the tool ready for prime time. Today, the tool, our 6PA software system, is an awesome success. It has been cited by *Monster.com* and others as an example of innovation and disruption in employee-performance software. Rather than owning only a portion of it had we taken venture capitalist funding, we own 100 percent of it. Clients of ours inquire all the time to see how we built it and to ask if we could build something similar for them. In the next few years, we plan to bring it to market, and I still maintain that it will be a commercially viable tool.

This is an example of one of the many doubters I've encountered in my career. All I can say to them is "thank you." Through constant innovation, self-reflection and work ethic, I was able to turn their doubts into accomplishments.

LESSON #42: EULOGY OVER RESUME

In 2014, I heard the speech that changed my life.

I was at a crossroads in my career. Our company was doing great. Revenues were higher than ever before, our staff was growing, we were starting to recruit top-notch talent, and bigger and better customers were signing with us. We were getting ready to move into a brand-new office in the neighborhood of my dreams. After years of blood, sweat and tears, our little company that started out of my basement was finally getting the recognition we deserved.

Larger and more established firms began expressing interest in acquiring us. It was the first time in my life that I was faced with a decision like this.

For my wife and me, with three young daughters at home, selling our company would present an opportunity for us to change our lives financially. Neither she nor I grew up with tons of money, and this was the first time in our lives where we could provide our family with long-term stability and financial comfort.

"Do I sell or do I keep building?" I asked myself.

I knew further scale would come at a hefty price, as I had gotten a taste of how challenging it was from the previous five years of growing our company. Sleepless nights, unthinkable stress, countless tests of will and other big sacrifices were in order if I decided to keep scaling.

With one signature on the dotted line, I could make all of it go away. Talk about tempting.

Indeed, I was at a crossroads.

Then I heard the speech that changed my life.

Legendary columnist David Brooks gave a TED Talk about the concept of people who live for their resume versus those who live for their eulogy. As he explained, they were two completely different mindsets with different philosophies and ways of approaching life. Indeed, the vast majority of people concentrated on living their lives with their resumes in mind.

Even though his speech (which was personal and spiritual in nature) was completely different from how I interpreted it (through a business lens), I saw it as a sign from above and applied it to my own career journey.

How did I want to approach the future of my career? Did I want to approach it based on the short term, continuing to see our company as merely a means to an end for my family, my loved ones and our employees (the "Resume")? Or did I want to approach it based on the long term, challenging myself to grow our business based on how we will be remembered decades from now when we all look back and reflect on the memories (the "Eulogy")?

It was at that moment that my mind was made up.

I called back some of the larger suitors that wanted to acquire us and told them to hold their checkbooks. We were going to keep building. We were going to build to be remembered, not to fade into oblivion. We were going to build toward a eulogy that would be beautifully written when it was all said and done.

This was a transformational moment in my career, and one on which I look back to this very day. Several years have passed since this moment. I would be lying if I said that I didn't think about it regularly and question whether I made the right decision.

Since that turning point, our company has kept growing. Our people are amazing. Our culture and environment are as warm and rewarding as I had envisioned from day one. Year after year, we make significant strides and improvements to our business.

We have done some phenomenal things since that year of self-reflection in 2014. I am very proud of all this.

However, it has come at an incredible price. It has come at the expense of gut-wrenching decisions, personal sacrifice, and constant moments of doubt and fear. Many nights I have stayed up and cursed that speech. Maybe I would've been better off had I not listened to it in the first place. Perhaps I should've sold the company when I had the chance. Who knows what would've happened if I never came across the speech?

Then I think back to the purpose of the "Eulogy" philosophy and I am reassured that it was the right move. The "Eulogy" approach to your career requires a completely different mindset. It forces you to make decisions not based on the realities of today but based on how you want things to be when the final chapter is written.

Even though things can get chaotic on a day-to-day basis in the workplace, I remind myself that each day we are writing another line in what will be a beautiful and fulfilling eulogy when all is said and done.

Unfortunately, there are no guarantees in our careers. There is no guarantee that I made the right choice. But as long as I keep running our business, I am going to approach every day with unwavering conviction that our eulogy will bring pride and fulfillment to all of those who are there to see us go out.

Make no mistake, running our business with the "Eulogy" mindset has not been without strife — headaches, hair loss, butterflies and fatigue. You name it and I've felt it.

But boy, am I glad that I've chosen the "Eulogy" approach. I wouldn't have it any other way.

LESSON #43: LESSONS FROM MOM

What kind of son would I be if I didn't mention the lessons I've picked up from my mother that have served me well in my career?

When I was growing up, my mother and I would talk all night long over coffee and pastries at the kitchen table. Years later, when I started our company, my mother would pick me up at 6 o'clock every morning and drive me into the office. She was well into her retirement at that point at had no reason to wake up so early. She just wanted to spend some time with her son. I might not have been a bigwig Wall Street CEO, but I had a better chauffeur than any of them!

These moments were like flashbacks to my childhood. She would inspire me with words of wisdom and encouragement on those early morning drives just like she did when I was a kid during those late-night talks.

As our company has gotten bigger and my schedule has become more demanding, those morning drives have become fewer and fewer. It's one of my biggest regrets. However, the messages from those morning drives and nights at the kitchen table still serve as some of the most meaningful entrepreneurial lessons I've learned.

Here are four lessons that I learned from mom:

It's all about balancing extremes. My mother showed me at an early age that the biggest obstacle standing in the way of accomplishing dreams in your career is how comfortable you are operating in the "extreme" zone.

If there's one thing that I've learned since our company was founded it's that successful entrepreneurship boils down to the ability to manage the constant tug of extreme, contrasting emotions.

On one hand, immense fear and loneliness consume you, knowing that everything you've built can crumble in the blink of an eye. On the other hand, extreme ambition and optimism energize you, reinforcing your conviction that the vision you've created can reach its ultimate destination.

Every entrepreneur struggles with this constant tug of extremes.

My mother helped me navigate through periods of extreme pain in life — the death of a sibling, life-threatening health scares, and others. She helped me get through these moments with incredible strength and selflessness. Through all of the pain, my mother never thought about herself. She put me first and showed me that out of extreme pain, beautiful moments can emerge. Following this period of adversity early on in life, I met my wife, started a business, and found renewed spirit and motivation.

The "extreme" zone that every entrepreneur inevitably faces in business is something that I was prepared for thanks to lessons I learned from mom.

Inspiration comes from within. My mother wouldn't know the difference between a P&L and P&G. She probably thinks NASDAQ is a space invention and a KPI is something that can be found on the dashboard of an automobile.

My mother has never hired an employee, scrutinized an org chart or worried about a sales quota. She has never stepped foot in corporate America for one day.

Yet, she is the reason behind any modicum of success that I've achieved in business. She didn't do this through teaching me about P&Ls or helping me manage a workforce.

She did this through something far more powerful than any of those things.

She did this through the *gift of inspiration.*

On the first day of our company's existence, my mother wrote me a greeting card: "Enjoy the journey. If you inspire others, you will be a winner no matter what happens."

I keep that card on my desk to this day. As the years continue to pass and the ink from the card fades, the meaning behind those words has become more and more evident to me. My mother always made inspiration the most important part of my everyday life, and it has helped me in business.

Never forget your roots. My mother was the daughter of immigrants, a poor family who came to the United States and made ultimate sacrifices to put future generations like myself in a position to realize our dreams. Her parents never drove a car, never owned a home, and never spoke our language.

My mother fought her way through comas and car accidents, through cramped bedrooms shared with her sister, through breast cancer and through countless other tests of adversity. She never once complained about any of it. My mother bestowed upon me the importance of hard work and the power of fighting.

Most importantly, my mother taught me to never forget my roots.

When I started our company and was deciding on names, it was a no-brainer for me to name it after the street on which my grandparents lived after they immigrated from Italy to the United States. This has served as a reminder every day that no matter how great the success or how painful the failure, the one constant is that we always remember our roots.

Of all our business accomplishments, perhaps the one that I'm most proud of is that our values, culture and heritage are deeply rooted in the fabric of our every move. At every step of the way, we've managed to maintain a pride and respect for our roots and our underdog journey. We have a story, we have a tradition, and we have an appreciation for the grind that has unified us.

This traces its roots back to one simple message from my mother: Be proud of who you are and where you come from.

The power of belief and loyalty. My mother has believed in me my entire life. Even during moments when I gave her no reason to believe, she refused to give up on me.

Growing up, I can remember weeks, even months, of giving my mother the cold-shoulder treatment over petty disagreements. I can remember senseless and immature decisions that I made as a kid, such as skipping school to roll dice and playing the role of neighborhood bookie before the days of online betting.

Through all the pain and frustration I put my mother through, she stood by me with the unwavering loyalty and patience that only a mother could have. Even through my darkest displays of selfishness, my mother was right there by my side, knowing that I would come around eventually.

The power of believing in someone and standing by him or her should never be underestimated, particularly as you navigate through your career.

Some people learn about the power and importance of these lessons after they take the corner office.

For me, I've understood them my entire life. I guess I'm just lucky. For that I thank my mother.

LESSON #44: LOOK OUTSIDE YOUR INDUSTRY

I have found that some of the most successful ideas I've conceived in my career have come from looking at people and companies outside of my industry.

Winning ideas are usually fueled by creativity and intelligent risk taking, as I have learned. And sometimes the best place to find them is in a different business altogether, from innovators that have nothing to do with your profession at all.

Our best experiments as a company have happened when we've looked at aspirational brands from other industries, studied their playbooks, then put our own, unique twist on something they've done.

In December 2015, I was scrambling frantically to find a holiday gift for my wife. It was Christmas Eve, and as I typically do, I waited until the very last minute before doing my Christmas shopping. There was a particular handbag I was looking for, and unsurprisingly, every store I called was out of stock. I searched far and wide, but many stores wouldn't even pick up my call.

Finally, I put a call into the local Nordstrom at the Westchester Mall in White Plains, New York. Just like other retailers on Christmas Eve, the store was packed with last-minute shoppers. I was unable to get someone live on the phone, so I left a message for the handbag department. I figured it was an exercise in futility and that nobody would call me back.

Much to my surprise, I received a call back from a friendly and knowledgeable customer service representative within minutes. She directed me to a nearby Nordstrom that had the handbag I was looking for and went so far as to put it on hold for me.

"Now, that's customer service!" I thought. "We should implement something like this for our business."

Later on, I called Nordstrom's corporate office to share the story of the positive experience I'd had. During that conversation, I learned that the retailer has a rapid-response policy requiring that customer service representatives immediately return customers' messages.

Coincidentally, as all of this was happening, our company was looking to implement practices that would improve our responsiveness to our own customers. We looked at various practices Nordstrom implemented in order to create a culture of rapid response, including my own experience while Christmas shopping.

That's how our "6-Minute Response" policy came about. We tend to do everything in "sixes" at N6A, so we took Nordstrom's policy and then put our own twist on it to make it unique to our culture. As a result, any client who sends us a message gets a response from our account management team within six minutes.

Years later, this has become an important part of the fabric and nature of our customer service culture, and something that our staff and customers have gotten behind.

It all started by looking outside of our industry and then putting our own twist on it.

LESSON #45: "E" COMES BEFORE "A"

"A" might come before "E" in the dictionary, but not in management.

That is, *Earn* comes before *Ask*.

As a manager, the most successful relationships I've had with my subordinates have been when they've earned things *before* they've asked for them.

Anytime I've acquiesced when someone has asked for something *before* they've earned it, it has been a guaranteed recipe for failure.

Want that big promotion?

Think you're ready for that hefty pay increase?

Want that fancy new job title on your business card?

Earn it before you *ask* for it.

I've learned that rewards should be handed down, and handed down generously at that, but only when it has been *earned* based on merits and performance. Whenever I've rewarded someone based on speculation or as a prepayment on future expectations, it has crashed and burned quickly.

Anytime I've rewarded someone who *asked* before he or she *earned*, it has led to a disastrous outcome. In these situations, I've typically placed people in roles they weren't ready for in the first place, given them titles that were inflated relative to the value they drove to our company, or set the wrong precedent for others who actually earned the right to the same rewards based on their merits.

Now, here's the *most* important part about this lesson.

A good manager won't let it get to the "ask" stage. A good manager will reward the performer as soon as it has been earned. Once the performance and results have merited the big promotion, job title or pay increase, a good manager will be proactive and give out the reward *before* the subordinate gets a chance to ask for it.

Herein lies the healthiest and most productive manager-to-subordinate relationship that I've observed in my career. The subordinate earns something based on merits and performance, and the manager immediately rewards the subordinate before it gets to the point where he or she even has to ask for it.

We've given out more than 100 promotions, and I estimate that 80 percent of them have been merit-based and followed the *earn before ask* principle. In almost all of those cases, the people who got promoted went on to achieve great things in their new roles and had a positive impact on our company. They appreciated the opportunity, they were grateful that they were given the rewards before they had to ask for them, and they were more adequately prepared to succeed once they stepped into their new roles or titles.

In the 20 percent of instances when we've given promotions when they've been *asked before earned,* we've experienced completely different outcomes. In each of these situations, the employee wasn't ready for the new promotion to begin with, which had a ripple effect across the company. It typically led to higher employee attrition rates, improper training and mentorship, inefficient use of time and resources, and performance breakdowns across other departments.

As a manager, it's not easy to have the tough conversations, but you need to have them. If employees ask for something before you feel they've earned it, you owe it to them to tell them the truth. If you feel employees have earned something, it's on you to reward them before they even get a chance to ask for it.

Don't let the dictionary fool you when it comes to management. "E" definitely comes before "A."

LESSON #46: THE "IT'S NOT PERSONAL, IT'S BUSINESS" LIE

Let's dispel a longtime fallacy.

It's not personal, it's business.

If you're like me, I'm sure you've heard that time and time again in your career.

"Matt, we don't want to hire your firm. Don't worry, it's not personal, it's business."

"Matt, we don't want to work on your team. Don't worry, it's not personal, it's business."

"Matt, we don't want to invest in your company. Don't worry, it's not personal, it's business."

Just like me, I'm sure you've been told at some point in your career that you or your services are no longer wanted. Whether it's by a former employer, a prospective employer, a customer or someone else, chances are you've heard this before. You can't tell me that you didn't take it personally in some way, even if it was deep down inside and you didn't show it externally.

Relax, this doesn't make you unprofessional. It doesn't make you a loser. It doesn't make you weak. It makes you a *human being*.

The notion that you can't be both personal *and* professional in your approach to your craft is nonsense.

Our businesses and our careers are absolutely personal. In some way, shape or form, they are reflections of who we are as people. They trigger very personal emotions and actions unlike almost anything else in our lives outside of our friends and family.

Sir Martin Sorrell once stated that "founder's connection" — the connection an entrepreneur has to his or her business — is the closest thing to childbirth a man can experience. I would have no way of confirming or denying what labor pains feel like, but I can certainly say that my business is the most personal thing in my life outside of my wife and kids. It has become a living, breathing form of life in many ways.

Therefore, I have no problem saying that business is very personal to me. Despite my best efforts, I've always found it difficult to separate natural, human emotions from my work.

What I've learned through the years is, rather than to pretend that business isn't personal, I embrace it and make it part of my approach to work. The way in which I manage people has more of a personal touch than a strictly professional but emotionless approach. Of course, I try to walk the line and make sure that I'm never overstepping into the unprofessional zone.

Some of the most galvanizing moments I've had with my colleagues have come not inside but outside the office, through outings, family gatherings and other events that are personal in nature.

Of course, when you have a personal touch but are faced with the inevitable tough decisions that come with running a business — letting employees go, restructuring departments, cutting back on budgets — conversations can be particularly difficult. This is one of the downsides of taking a personal approach, but I've learned to live with it. After all, this is who I am, and I'd rather be true to myself than pretend to be someone I'm not.

Next time someone tells you it's not personal, it's business, you should tell them the truth. Your career *is* personal, and you're proud to say it.

LESSON #47: FIND A SAFE HAVEN

There's nothing remarkable about North 6th Avenue in Mount Vernon, New York. Just a mile north of the Bronx border, the houses along North 6th Avenue are all two- and three-family homes occupied by working-class people. The neighborhood has changed quite a bit from when I was a child.

Every time I think of North 6th Avenue, it conjures up fond memories of my childhood. Shopping with my grandparents at the nearby market, visiting my grandmother's food stand at the Italian feast at Our Lady of Victory church, surprise visits to my mother's classroom down the block, countless weekends and nights on my grandparents' couch.

When I was growing up, the neighborhood had produced many examples of real, working-class success stories. Puff Daddy, Denzel Washington, David Chase and many others all hailed from the neighborhood and its immediate surroundings.

Even though I grew up in a more well-to-do neighborhood a few miles away, I spent so many days and weekends on North 6th Avenue that I practically lived there. Both sets of my grandparents lived in the area. My parents grew up there along with so many of my cousins, aunts and uncles. One of my grandfathers worked in the local parks department. My mother was a city employee for nearly 40 years, working just down the block.

The neighborhood was an enclave for hard-working, honest, blue-collar people who aspired to achieve great things but didn't have the luxury of taking shortcuts to get there. This in itself would become great inspiration for me when I later embarked on my career journey.

There was a special warmth, vibrance and hope on the block that no longer seems to radiate in the neighborhood like it once did.

Despite all of this, on many weekends I still find myself taking the short drive over from my house to North 6th Avenue.

There's really no reason for me to be there anymore. My grandparents haven't lived there for years, and my family has all left for greener pastures across New York City, Westchester and Long Island. My grandfather passed away in 2004, and my grandmother has been in a nursing home, suffering from dementia, for several years now.

Yet, I still drive by their old house often. I've found it to be a safe haven for me when I've needed it the most in my career. Well before I started our company, I would head over there when I was faced with adversity in my career. I remember getting butterflies in my stomach before I started my first job out of college. I can still remember the weight of anxiety that I felt when I moved into my first management role. And of course, I also remember the pressures and uncertainties when deciding whether to start my own company, before I eventually made the decision to go for it.

Through all of these moments, there was North 6th Avenue.

Even though there's nothing particularly remarkable about the block nowadays, it continues to serve a purpose for me, providing me with a feeling of hope and calmness when I need it most in my career. It has always conjured up good memories for me and has been a place where I could go to remind me what my career journey is all about.

The truth is, each of us has our own North 6th Avenue, a place we can visit when we need it the most.

If you can't think of your career safe haven immediately, give it some time. I bet you'll be able to find it if you give it some thought. Once you do, take a stroll there. I'm sure it'll help bring perspective and purpose to your career, just like North 6th Avenue has provided me.

LESSON #48: COMPLACENCY WILL KILL YOUR CAREER

In early 2011, I learned the hard way that complacency is kryptonite for your career.

At that time, our average client retainer was at the extreme low end of our industry. Our book of business was predominately unknown start-ups that engaged with us on short-term trial contracts. We were constantly on the hunt for talent and found ourselves having to convince candidates why they should come work for an unknown start-up. As a small, brand-new operation, I found myself wearing many hats.

I was the CEO by title only. In reality, I was responsible for doing a little bit of everything. Just like most entrepreneurs just starting out, I was doing it all in those days. I was the rainmaker responsible for bringing in new accounts. I was the primary account manager servicing our clients day-to-day. And I had my hand in everything else you could think of, including payroll, logistics, human resources and operations.

As you can imagine, when Xoom knocked on our door in the summer of 2011, I jumped at the opportunity. Back then, Xoom was one of the hottest tech start-ups on the planet. It was an early innovator in the online payments category and would later be acquired by PayPal for more than $1 billion, making this lesson an even more painful one for me to learn.

Xoom was introduced through one of our mutual clients and was looking for a small, scrappy firm to take on a quick seasonal project. If the company did well on the project, it would lead to a very lucrative annual contract, changing the trajectory of our business.

I worked tirelessly to make sure we won the competitive pitch process, including flying out to Xoom's headquarters in San Francisco and presenting to its management team. A few weeks later, we received great news from Xoom: We got the project. I was elated!

This was our big chance to grow our client retainers to the next level and to step into the big leagues with larger and more sustainable accounts. All we had to do was perform well during the trial project and we would be set. We would then parlay this short-term relationship into a huge, annual contract with a hefty fee attached to it, and we'd be off to the races as a firm.

However, I got complacent. Rather than hustling just as hard to service the account as I did to win it, I took my foot off the pedal once the company signed on the dotted line. I had assumed that, once it signed with us for the trial project, we would be on easy street and the renewal would be a foregone conclusion. That was a stupid assumption.

Forget about "servicing" the account — I should have been heads-down doing everything I could to "over-service" the account, impressing the client so much during the trial project that it would have no choice but to renew.

Instead, I only serviced the account moderately and focused the rest of my time on running other aspects of our business. It was evident to the client that the hustle and hunger I showed to win the business did not extend to my servicing of the account.

Xoom fired me quickly, choosing not to renew its contract once the project expired. More importantly, I squandered a golden opportunity to change the destiny of our firm.

Had I not been complacent during the service phase of the account, I'm convinced that we would've converted the project to a recurring contract, and we would've been along for the ride when PayPal acquired Xoom a few years later. Who knows, maybe we would've even won the global PayPal account as a result.

From that point forward, I vowed to never get complacent in any aspect of our business, whether it was sales, service or anything else.

Complacency will kill you, as I learned the hard way in early 2011. Avoid it like the plague.

LESSON #49: PROOF THAT EXCUSES STINK

Here's a calm and soothing ancient proverb that I remember hearing years ago:

"Opinions are like assholes. Everybody's got one and everyone thinks each other's stinks."

In the workplace, "opinions" can easily be replaced with "excuses" and the saying works just as well. That's right, excuses *stink* in the workplace. Excuses are a mammoth waste of time and energy that could just as easily be redirected toward something that will move the needle for your career, like *execution*.

To prove this theory, I tested out a novel concept for a month back in 2012. Every time I caught myself making an excuse or overheard someone else making one in the office, I jotted it down. I assigned an amount of time that I assumed was spent on each excuse. Between coming up with the excuse, communicating the excuse and discussing the excuse among peers, the average excuse resulted in approximately 20 minutes of time wasted.

At the end of the month, I tallied them up: 45 excuses, for a grand total of 900 minutes. That equaled 15 hours of time wasted on excuses in that month alone! I needed to own up to my own contributions, too. I was responsible for nearly 10 excuses myself.

Imagine what might've happened if we had applied all that time to executing for our clients or to improving collaboration with our peers. Imagine how much better off our team would have been as a result. Instead of focusing on execution, we wasted 15 hours, more than one-third of a work week, on *excuses*.

The next month, I tested out the theory again, except this time I only kept track of my own excuses rather than everyone else's. I was committed to cutting back on my excuse time and redirecting it to more productive activities that contributed to the growth of the team and business.

As a result, my excuses the following month dropped down to just three, meaning just one hour was wasted. During that same month, I also brought in more sales than I had in any previous three-month span and our client attrition rate was better than it had ever been. Most importantly, I noticed that everyone else in the office didn't have as many excuses as they did the previous month. Their excuse rates dropped presumably because they took a cue from me as the leader of the company. As my excuse rate dropped, so did theirs. Although I didn't keep track of their excuse tally, there was a noticeable downtick from the previous month.

From that point forward, I realized how much of a time waster and energy sucker excuses were. It's human nature to make excuses, and it's unrealistic to assume your people will never make them. However, the more conscious you can be about the time that you spend on excuses, the better off you're going to be as a professional. The time you spend coming up with excuses, communicating them to your boss or subordinate and then discussing them with your peers is distracting you from putting the time to use in a more productive way, one that can advance your career.

Excuses really *stink*, and this is the proof. I'd much rather spend that time on execution.

LESSON #50: BE AN ENERGY ADDICT

As I've advanced in my career, I've learned to become a total energy addict. I refuse to surround myself in the workplace with people who don't exude up-tempo, positive energy and transfer it over to me. Don't get me wrong, I'm not talking about hyperkinetic, bounce-off-the-wall energy. I'm talking about people who have the ability to transfer positive energy from one person to the next. And I want them to hold me just as accountable for transferring this energy over to them.

I've become such an energy addict that every aspect of our office needs to exude excited, upbeat energy at all times.

Let me set the stage for what hits you as soon as you get off the elevator in our office.

Music is playing, not too loud but loud enough so that you can hear and feel it. People are talking, not in an obnoxious way but in a collaborative and constructive way. Neon lights are on, not in a blinding way but in a noticeably illuminating way. Television screens are switched on, bodies are in motion, food is on display and laughter is abounding. There is a palpable buzz and a feeling of adrenaline that continually flows from the start of the day to the end of the day.

That is *winning* energy right there.

In the old days, this used to be the type of energy that I *wanted* in the office. Nowadays, it has become the energy that I *need* in the office. I can't function anymore unless there is this type of energy around me.

In my experience, people focus on the emotional energy in the workplace, but often forget to concentrate on the *physical* energy. What is the energy in the office? What is the atmosphere? What is the environment like? Every detail counts.

The physical energy is every bit as important as the emotional energy. Your workplace is the stage on which you perform each day. How can you perform at your peak if the energy in the office is flat and dry? The energy needs to scream "yes we can!" It needs to project optimism, collaboration and pace.

I really enjoy coming into the office. It took a while to get our energy to this level, but I know now that from the second I get off the elevator in the morning until the second I leave at night, I'm going to be surrounded by great energy at every corner. From the energy in the people to the energy in the office, it's a wonderful feeling. The positive energy is transmitted by everyone and to everyone.

Energy has become an addiction for me, but a good kind. I wish my standards for workplace energy had been higher earlier in my career, because I've seen the positive impact — on my performance, my motivation, my confidence level and my sense of accomplishment — ever since I became an addict.

When it comes to workplace energy, you should become an energy addict. Don't make any compromises. It will change your career.

LESSON #51: THE FARM, THE BARN AND SUNLIGHT

In *The Great Pearls of Wisdom,* author Bangambiki Habyarimana writes that "opportunity and risk come in pairs." No statement has ever been truer in my own dealings with risk assessment over the course of my career.

If your career is anything like mine, many of your greatest opportunities will be born from risk. Your successes and failures will come down to your ability to assess, tolerate and ultimately *decide* on which risks to take and when to take them.

Here is my point of view on risk assessment: Don't be afraid to move the barn to find sunlight, but never, ever bet the farm.

This has been my guiding principle when it comes to risk assessment as my career has evolved. As an entrepreneur, you need to have a stomach for risk tolerance. Everyone knows that nothing great can be achieved without taking risk.

However, what often gets lost in the risk discussion is the importance of risk *assessment* — how to decide whether or not to take the risk in the first place, when to take the risk, and when to cut your losses if the risk isn't working out.

The farm, the barn and sunlight principle has served me very well in my dealings with risk assessment.

If I feel something can make our company better or make me a better CEO — a new investment, a potential acquisition, a test experiment, a structural change within our organization, a new initiative or product upgrade — I'm generally open to taking the risk and comfortable testing it out. However, if the risk could be damaging to our company in a material way, I won't take it.

In other words, I have no problem moving the *barn* around to find *sunlight*, but I will never, ever bet the *farm*.

You can live with failed experiments if they have a short-term impact to your career or business. You can simply chalk them up to one of the thousands of losses and lessons that you will learn over the course of your career. This is the "barn" metaphor.

However, you can't live with the failed experiments that could put you out of business or out of a job. This the "farm" metaphor.

Over the years, I've taken hundreds, maybe thousands, of risks that have had losing outcomes. These risks have resulted in millions of dollars of losses, countless hours of lost time and other collateral damage.

Following are a few examples of risks I've taken that have come with losing outcomes. In 2012, we spent more than three months and hired multiple consultants to test out the launch of a sports and entertainment management practice. In 2017, we spent a few million dollars of our own capital to acquire a company and open an office in Toronto that we ended up shutting a few years later. In 2019, we spent considerable time and money to build a software product that we never took to market.

However, through all of the failed experiments, I'm still standing and our business has remained squarely on the tracks.

This happened because no risk that I have ever taken has been a "bet the farm" risk, where the end result would be game over. Through all of the risks I mention above, we knew the worst case would be a write-off, a short-term loss, or wasted time and opportunity costs. These are certainly not insignificant considerations without damaging effects, but they are not crippling effects from which you cannot recover.

Nowadays, anytime I sit down at the table with my management team and assess the risk that comes with a potential decision, we'll go straight to the farm question: "If we take this risk, what is the worst-case scenario? Can we lose the farm?" If the answer is yes, then we will never move forward. If the answer is no, then we'll look deeper and ask ourselves the next layer of questions ("How much time is involved? "What is the potential reward?"), but we'll generally err on the side of taking the risk more times than not.

Next time you assess whether to take a potential risk in your career, lean on *the farm, the barn and sunlight* principle. If you're simply moving the barn around to find sunlight, go for it. But never, *ever* bet the farm.

LESSON #52: BE "BENSOCAL"

In May 2015, this was the first monthly performance report and feedback assessment I gave to my future Chief Operating Officer Daniela Mancinelli:

"I need to see more Bensonhurst, less SoCal."

It was short and simple, and it was the last time I ever had to deliver this feedback to her. From that point forward, she has been *BenSoCal* in every sense.

Before I get into what it means to be *BenSoCal,* you need to understand the story behind my hiring Daniela.

Just a month earlier, I brought her in to help manage a portfolio of client accounts. We had strong business-to-business and technology account management experience, but Daniela had a consumer background, and I thought the diversity would help improve our client service offering. I knew from the very first time I met her that she would be special.

It was evident to me immediately that she had unique traits that would carry her far in her career. She had incredible empathy and a burning ambition to go along with a uniquely global perspective, a high level of integrity and a balanced temperament that would serve her well in the inevitable high-pressure moments that come with operating a business. She had a passion and curiosity for people and problem-solving that was incredibly rare and hard to find in an employee. She also yearned for feedback and self-improvement.

Most people hide from challenges, but Daniela confronted them head-on with a fighting spirit. Most people get frustrated by the people management part of a job, but Daniela embraced it. Most people are comfortable with the status quo, but Daniela challenged it.

All of this was evident to me within minutes of meeting with her for the first time. She was in her early 30s and I viewed her as someone who could grow with the company for a long time to come.

There was only one big problem: The role I was interviewing her for was *not* the role I had envisioned for her. I saw her much more as a leader of people and as an agent for growth than I did as a mid-level client services manager, which was what we needed at the time.

Fast-forward five years later, and for all the bets I've gotten wrong, Daniela was one that I got 100 percent right, and I'm proud of that. She is in the exact role I had envisioned. She operates masterfully, sees through blind spots and works alongside me as we grow our business.

She is well liked and well respected by all, and she has brought another dimension to our company as we have scaled.

What was it that I saw in her and how did I know she was someone who was worth betting on? The answer is simple:

BenSoCal.

That's right. She had a lot of *BenSoCal* in her.

BenSoCal = Bensonhurst + Southern California.

Bensonhurst, Brooklyn — before it was yuppified with creme brûlée lattes and quinoa bowls — was an enclave for working-class people. People who put in an honest day's work, brought a lunch pail to their job and a blue-collar toughness to their craft.

Southern California, meanwhile, is about as far away from Bensonhurst as you can get, both literally and figuratively. Sunshine, waves, smiles and a carefree spirit.

You see, both the qualities of Bensonhurst and those of SoCal will serve you well in your career. However, very few people actually have both (take it from someone who wouldn't know SoCal if it hit him over the head with a surfboard). Usually, people are disproportionately skewed to one side or the other, either fiercely rugged but lacking the emotional quotient (EQ) required to relate to their people (Bensonhurst) or eternally optimistic but lacking the pragmatism required to get the most out of their people (SoCal).

BenSoCal people are rare to find, and when you find them, you need to hold onto them. They bring a unique balance of old-world toughness along with a warm and welcoming style that people gravitate toward. They also know how to read situations perfectly and when to wear the Bensonhurst hat versus the SoCal hat. The end result is usually a perfect performance optimization yield.

As you hire people, particularly ones you view as critical to the long-term vision of your business, place your bets on those who display *BenSoCal* qualities. Trust me on this one. It has served me very well.

Be *BenSoCal.*

LESSON #53: BE PATIENT AND PLAY THE LONG GAME

For someone who runs his own business and clearly is not in the job market, I get an unusually high volume of calls from headhunters and executive recruiters with job offers.

I don't know why they think I'm looking for a job, but I must admit, some of the calls have been tempting.

My ultimate career goal is to run a large, global organization. Of course, my aspiration is for that organization to be N6A, having built it to scale with our own people and our own capital. But the fact remains that, when all is said and done, I want to challenge myself to run a global company.

This is why some of those calls from headhunters have gotten my attention. Some of the offers have been for CEO and other leadership positions where I would stand to make a considerably higher salary than I do now. And yet, I've said no to all of them, no matter how attractive they may have been.

Why have I said no? Because I'm trying to *be patient and play the long game.*

Even though the short-term advantages of some of the offers have been enticing — a higher income, more upside, bigger and better resources to work with — they don't get me to where I want to be in the long run.

In 2018, I was approached by a large media company with a global footprint. It was based overseas and was looking for a new lead to run its North American operations. The position would report directly to the CEO, who is based in the company's headquarters in Europe, and indirectly to the board of directors.

At the time, this company was struggling with recruiting, sales and employee morale in its North American office. It was losing clients and talent to its U.S.-based competitors. It was faced with myriad challenges and was looking for a younger executive with a fresh perspective and leadership style and the energy to change the culture of its North American operation.

I was flattered to be on the company's shortlist of candidates and to be in serious consideration for the role. The company went so far as to offer me a lucrative, long-term contract and was willing to acquire our company at a generous valuation based on revenue rather than EBITDA, which is very rare in the business services category. Typically, revenue valuations are reserved for hot tech companies, unicorn start-ups and companies in sexy, high-growth categories, not in business services categories such as marketing and public relations.

Naturally, I listened to the offer and talked it over with my wife, my management team and other people in my inner circle.

In the end, I politely declined. Had I accepted the offer, my earnings potential would have grown by nearly three times what I was making running my own business and I would have had access to virtually unlimited resources. Additionally, the challenge of inheriting a struggling operation and turning it into a success story was intriguing to me.

Throughout the process, I kept reminding myself of my long-term career goal. No matter how intriguing and lucrative this opportunity was, it simply didn't fit in with my long-term goal. The younger, more impatient version of myself would have probably jumped at the opportunity. However, in time, I've learned to be more patient and to play the long game. Had I accepted the offer, I would have been wealthier, but also further away from achieving my goals. That just didn't sit well with me. I'd rather be less wealthy and closer to achieving my goals.

If something doesn't fit in with my long-term career goal, I've learned to say no, no matter how difficult it is to exercise the restraint and discipline to do so.

Everyone has a long-term goal they'd like to accomplish before their career is over. Based on my own learnings, my advice would be to make short-term decisions based on how close they get you to achieving your long-term goal. At times, this means that you're going to have to avoid temptation, whether it's the lure of more money, more responsibility or more resources.

Remember, eyes on the prize. *Be patient and play the long game.*

LESSON #54: ALWAYS MANAGE ON OFFENSE, NEVER ON DEFENSE

When it comes to management, I've learned that you should always be on *offense*. Strong managers are always the lead dance partner, never the follower. They take the lead on the relationship with their subordinates, dictating the pace, operating from a position of strength, and anticipating the next step before their partner takes it. Anytime I've ever managed from a position of defense rather than offense, it has led to disastrous outcomes.

Common examples of manager-to-subordinate situations I've encountered through the years have included decisions on compensation increases, promotions, workload allocation, customer relationship management, and choices around pairing subordinates. The truth is, an effective manager should be on offense when managing each of these decisions.

Here are examples of how an *offensive* versus *defensive* manager would approach situations:

Compensation increases. One who manages on *offense* is constantly running proper checks to make sure subordinates are compensated relative to the value they bring to the team. They make adjustments to subordinates' compensation, or communicate proactively with employees in cases where budget or process restrictions prevent such adjustments. Those who manage on *defense* wait for subordinates to come to them for a compensation request, then make decisions based on the fear of losing an employee rather than on the value an employee is bringing to the team. A manager on *offense* would rather let an employee walk than make a compensation decision based on the fear of them leaving.

Promotions. One who manages on *offense* will communicate proactively and draw up clear steps to show a subordinate how he or she can earn that big promotion. Most importantly, once subordinates have earned the right to a promotion based on their performance, the manager on *offense* will give it to them. Meanwhile, those who manage on *defense* are ambiguous and unclear with subordinates about the steps they must take to earn a promotion. Managers on *defense* deal with promotions reactively and are forced to make decisions on their heels, after a subordinate confronts them about it.

Workload allocation. Those who manage on *offense* know the capacity threshold of their subordinates through a combination of strong instincts and objective data. Managers on *offense* assign workloads based on how they can optimize the efficiency of their subordinates. Those who manage on *defense* scale workload assignments up or back reactively, based on feedback from their subordinates only after they bring it to the manager's attention.

Team pairings. Those who manage on *offense* know their personnel better than anyone else, and will pair certain team members based on which pairings will deliver the best outcomes. One who manages on *defense* will pair those same team members based on fear and paranoia rather than how those subordinates will react to being on the same team.

Customer relationship management. One who manages on *offense* knows the needs of the customer and is anticipatory about the customer's needs. Those who manage on *defense* wait until the customer files a complaint, then reacts to the customer's needs.

I've found that whenever I've managed from a position of defense, it's been a guaranteed recipe for disaster. Some of the worst decisions I've made regarding employee compensation, personnel selection and customer management have been the result of managing from a position of defense instead of offense. Anytime I've managed on offense, it's been a completely different outcome, leading me to make smart and sound decisions, setting the right precedent for others in the organization, and always feeling a sense of control and ownership over my decisions.

Be honest and ask yourself if you're someone who manages on *offense* or *defense*. The winning ticket always lies on *offense*.

LESSON #55: CIRCLE THE TWO-JUMPERS

One of the unfortunate inevitabilities of management is that you are going to lose some of your people. Many of these people are going to be perfectly talented and gifted employees who decide to leave for one reason or another. Another unfortunate reality of management is that you can't invest *equally* in everybody. I wish this weren't the case, but the reality is that some talent commands special treatment and extra TLC when it comes to your investment of time, resources and money.

These are both unavoidable facts in the world of management. Here's another unavoidable fact:

You should never, ever lose a *two-jumper*.

What's a *two-jumper*? Allow me to explain.

Pick up a copy of your org chart or team roster and run through all the names. Then ask yourself the following question: "Who can I envision making two jumps up the org chart in the foreseeable future?" Circle their names with a thick, black Sharpie.

The *two-jumper* theory assumes that *anyone* can successfully make one jump up the org chart, but that very *few* can make two successful jumps in a relatively short period of time (three years or less).

Moving one notch up the org chart — from entry level to associate, associate to junior management, junior management to mid-level or senior management to C-suite — is not a rare or unique feat in the workplace. In fact, nearly 70 percent of people I've managed over the years have been able to make one jump. However, the success rate drops dramatically, all the way down to 20 percent, where two jumps are concerned.

Typically, this is because the skills required for an employee to do a job that's two levels above are completely different and oftentimes non-transferrable versus the skills that are most important in that person's current role.

Administrative skills and organization are critical at the entry level, but in time will that person be able to transition into a role that requires people management skills and that is two notches above their current role on the org chart? Tactical and creative skills are often the most important skills required at the associate level, but will that person eventually blossom into a strong, analytical manager and develop the ability to manage a P&L and other business-performance tools — knowledge that will be incumbent on them when they jump two levels into mid-level management?

Much to my surprise, the success rate for these *two-jumpers* is much lower than I would have ever imagined. I've observed that less than 20 percent have successfully been able to make two jumps in a window of three years or less.

What's the big takeaway?

Circle the *two-jumpers*, and never, *ever* let them get away.

I regularly go through this exercise with my management team. A few times each year, we'll sit down, review the org chart and ask ourselves this question: "Can we envision this entry-level employee becoming a manager in a few years, and can we envision this manager becoming part of the senior leadership team?" Once we make these assessments, we allocate a *disproportionate* investment of time, energy and resources to making sure we are doing everything we can to groom the *two-jumpers*.

Once you've identified a *two-jumper*, it's on you to do everything in your power to invest in this person so that he or she can successfully make the two jumps with your guidance and nurturing.

Of course, we don't get every call right. Sometimes those we envisioned being *two-jumpers* turn out to be one-jumpers, and people we correctly identify as *two-jumpers* wind up leaving before we get to see them in action at the next level.

I'm sure you have some *two-jumpers* on your team right now. Identify them. Circle their names. Invest in them.

LESSON #56: GROW THICKER SKIN

Here's a lesson I've learned through the years that will serve you well no matter where you are on your career journey, and no matter what your place is within the org chart:

Grow thicker skin.

You'd think someone like myself — New York-raised, the grandson of immigrants, the brother of a mentally disabled sibling, the son of a cancer survivor, a first-generation college graduate — wouldn't have a problem with having thick skin.

But that hasn't been the case at all.

In the decade since we started our business, I have let insecurity and doubt impact my decision-making on far too many occasions. Some of my biggest regrets and errors in judgment have come as a result of caring too much about what other people think.

The truth is, if you're the boss, you're going to piss some people off. Even if you're not the boss, you're probably going to piss some people off. You have to make tough decisions, you have to know when to trust your gut, and you have to be prepared to live with the consequences.

Whenever I have made a decision based on what people were going to think about me, it has not ended well.

Here's some data to support this lesson.

Hiring decisions. On 15 occasions over the years, I've hired people who, in my gut, I felt were inferior to their competing candidates, but I hired them anyway because I was worried about the reaction from the staff. Only five of those 15 hires made it past one year in the company, and none made it past two years. That's only a 33 percent success rate on new hires when I defied my better judgment and made decisions based on how I felt others would react.

Firing decisions. When faced with the decision to fire someone or move them to another position within the organization, my success rate is less than 10 percent. In other words, it is very rare that someone who was not performing in their current role has went on to perform well in a special role that I created for them. On the majority of these occasions, I made the decision *not* to fire the person because I was worried about what others would think rather than making the decision that I knew was right based on my instinct and experience.

Customer signings. I estimate that I've signed approximately 30 clients over the years that deep down I felt were bad for our business but that, against my better judgment, I signed anyway. I made most of these decisions because I either didn't have the cojones to tell the client I didn't want to do business with them or because I felt that we were too far along in the sales process to bail. Of these 30 clients, only 10 percent were retained for more than one year, 30 percent resulted in a tumultuous parting of ways, and 60 percent resulted in some sort of collateral damage such as employee retention, morale or long-term revenue impact.

The data speaks for itself. My advice would be to accept these unavoidable truths when you're in charge of making decisions. If you follow these unavoidable truths, you will find there's a much lower error rate in your decisions.

You're *not* going to get every decision right.

You're *not* going to get consensus on most decisions you make.

You *are* going to piss some people off when you make decisions.

Trust your gut, seek advice from people you respect, treat everyone fairly, and ultimately make the decision that you believe is right for your company, not the one that is right for your popularity score.

This will lead you to good places most of the time.

The thicker your skin is, the thicker the success rate of your decisions will be.

Grow thicker skin.

LESSON #57: HAVE A "STUFF HAPPENS" LINE ON YOUR P&L

During our first year in business, a $300,000 client account signed, terminated and stiffed us on the bill; multiple people who had accepted offers with us never showed up for work; a landlord held us hostage for a 50 percent rent increase after we already had a lease agreement in place; and our IT system crashed and burned suddenly, sending us into a panic and costing us loads of money to fix.

I learned immediately that, in business, well, *stuff happens*. The important lesson that I've learned through the years is that, you need to figure out a way to prepare for the unpredictable.

With this in mind, we created a "stuff happens" expense line on our P&L and in our budget beginning in 2011. Just as we account for expenses such as bad debt reserves, depreciation and monthly bonus accruals, and even as our Chief Financial Officer follows generally accepted accounting principles (GAAP), we built in a "stuff happens" line to prepare for the inevitable financial surprises we knew were coming our way but had no way of seeing.

After year one, we incurred approximately $100,000 in expenses that we were completely unprepared for as a result of the events listed above. Looking back, I'm quite shocked that we didn't go out of business or have to make drastic cuts to payroll in order to withstand the onslaught of unexpected expenses we incurred in our first year. This was on a revenue base of under $1 million. Using this as a formula, we began to set aside 10 percent of monthly revenues to account for "stuff happens" going forward.

As the years passed and our revenue kept growing, we saw that the percentage allocation for "stuff happens" expenditures was almost always unchanged. Every year it worked out to 10 percent, with a small variance. It was funny for me to see this on our budget, which was foreign to me to begin with since I had no financial background or acumen whatsoever. Right there below traditional, serious expense items such as payroll, rent, and travel and entertainment was a dedicated line, in bold, with the words "stuff happens." The truth is, even though it may sound funny, the "stuff happens" line became the most serious and carefully scrutinized of all of our expense items.

Even as we scaled our business and became more sophisticated in our accounting and expense methodology, we kept the "stuff happens" line intact as we found it served a real purpose. The line gave me a sense of comfort and preparation for the events that were impossible to prepare for.

Over time, whenever crazy financial surprises would land on my desk — last-minute flights to El Paso (we found the only client prospect in the world based in El Paso), expense slips from junior staff for "casual drinks" over Dom Perignon (they have better taste than I do!), back-up servers for when the computer system crashed — we were always prepared.

I wasn't *happy* whenever these events happened, but at least I was *prepared* for them. That alone gave me a sense of comfort and ease that helped me absorb these events. If it weren't for the "stuff happens" line, the financial impact of many of these unexpected expenses could have been catastrophic for our business, particularly in the early days before we had substantial cash reserves.

This wasn't the most *glamorous* lesson that I learned since starting our business, but it certainly was one of the most *necessary* ones.

Stuff happens. Don't worry about it. Just be prepared for it.

LESSON #58: MANAGEMENT BY STIMULATION VERSUS STABILITY

As we were putting the finishing touches on our first decade in business at the end of 2019, I conducted a study.

I went back and looked at 30 of my direct reports and a selection of other employees I had managed in one capacity or another over the past 10 years. They ranged in seniority, job title, personality and demographics. What I found fascinating as I reflected on my relationships with them was that they all had one thing in common: They were all looking for *stimulation*, *stability* or a combination of the two in the workplace.

The ones who were looking for stimulation were the ones who turned to the workplace as a source of inspiration. They were looking for meaning and purpose and wanted the workplace to serve as a smorgasbord from which they could quench their appetite for curiosity and self-development. They were comfortable with change, spontaneity and unpredictability, as long as it provided them with a source of stimulation in their careers.

The ones who were looking for stability were those who turned to the workplace as a steady and constant presence. They were looking for consistency and dependability, and wanted the workplace to serve as a domicile they could show up to every day, without change. They were comfortable operating within any guidelines in their day-to-day roles, as long as it provided them with a source of stability in their careers.

As I looked across each of these employees, I marked down which ones I felt were looking for stimulation, which ones were looking for stability, and which ones were looking for both. When I analyzed the data, the statistics were revealing to me.

Fourteen of the 30 employees were looking for stimulation, 13 were looking for stability, and three were looking for both. This meant that approximately 45 percent of employees were looking for stimulation — nearly the same percentage who sought stability — while 10 percent were looking for both.

Then I went back and studied the retention and success statistics for each of these employees. Specifically, I looked at which ones we retained for longer than the industry average at their respective job levels and the ones with whom I felt I had a successful management relationship. For each of the employees, I indicated whether I believed I took a "management by stimulation," "management by stability" or "management by both" approach. I then analyzed the retention and success statistics for each to see what the relationship was between my management style and their preferences.

This is where the numbers became startling.

Of the employees who exceeded the average industry retention rates and with whom I indicated that I had a successful management relationship, 21 were perfectly matched between my style and their preferences. In other words, these were employees who preferred to be managed by stimulation, stability or both, and I felt I did, in fact, manage them exactly as they preferred.

Eight of the employees fell short of average industry retention rates and were ones with whom I indicated that I had an unsuccessful management relationship. For all these employees, there was a directly opposite match between how I managed them and how they preferred to be managed. In other words, these were employees who preferred to be managed by stimulation, stability or both, and I felt I had failed to manage them as they preferred.

There was only one employee with whom I felt I had an unsuccessful management relationship that was a direct match between my style and this person's preference.

The key takeaway for me from this analysis was that I needed to ensure I understood what my subordinates were looking for in our management relationship out of the gate. Were they looking for stability, stimulation or both? I then needed to make sure I was, in fact, managing them with that approach in mind going forward.

The ones who wanted to be managed by stimulation were the ones for whom I would adopt a more idealistic management approach, oftentimes challenging them to step outside their comfort zone and make sure there was constant stimulation and spontaneity in our working relationship.

The ones who wanted to be managed by stability were the ones for whom I would adopt a more pragmatic management approach, oftentimes managing them through process, routine and structure.

Of course, I would adopt a mix of practices from both approaches for the few who wanted to be managed by both stimulation and stability.

Do your people prefer to be managed by stimulation, stability or both? Are you making adjustments to your style to make sure you're matched up properly with them? This was an important lesson that I learned thanks to running this analysis.

LESSON #59: FORESIGHT GETS YOU HIRED, HINDSIGHT GETS YOU FIRED

Both hindsight and foresight are important in the workplace, but here's an important lesson I've learned over the years:

Foresight gets you hired, but hindsight gets you fired.

Anytime I've uttered the words "if hindsight was 20/20" or have heard my direct reports say similar things to me, it has been as a response to a losing outcome. If I've heard the word "hindsight" 1,000 times, I would estimate that 990 of those times were in response to a client who fired us, a client who complained about botched service, a sales prospect whose account we lost or a talented employee who quit.

In my experience, hindsight is an important quality, but only because it enables you to study and learn from losses that occurred in the past. The fact remains that the outcome was a losing one, and you wouldn't have had to exercise hindsight in the first place if you had the foresight to get ahead of the outcome.

When I think of moments in my career when I've exercised hindsight, it conjures up difficult and sometimes painful, memories of lost accounts, lost employees and mindboggling lapses of judgment.

The truth is, you don't win because of hindsight, you lose because of it, and you use it to prevent losing again in the future. Having foresight, however, is where you *win*.

Whenever the word "foresight" has been used, it's been a preview of a winning outcome that's about to happen. Foresight is what gets you ahead of revenue opportunities, prevents clients from firing you, gives you a leg up on the competition and prevents you from losing that rockstar employee.

In time, I've found that everyone in the workplace has the ability to possess hindsight, but only very *few* have the ability to possess strong foresight.

Foresight is a quality that only a special few have — the ability to preempt, anticipate and act on instinct rather than on reflection. The best managers, the strongest-performing sales representatives and the most effective client service representatives in our company have been the ones who have exercised strong foresight. It's no surprise that these folks tend to be the ones who have made the most money, got promoted the fastest and received the highest client satisfaction ratings.

While foresight can be improved by leaning on data and exercising hindsight from past mistakes, I've found that the most proficient practitioners of foresight have an inherent ability and a keen nose for it. The trickiest part about foresight is that, in my experience, you either have it or you don't. Foresight is an extremely difficult trait to acquire. I've encountered only a handful of people who have entered their working relationship with me *lacking* a sense of foresight but have exited the working relationship *possessing* it.

While both foresight and hindsight are traits that I've found to be extremely valuable in my career, if I had to choose one I would choose foresight every day and twice on Sunday.

Foresight gets you *hired*, but hindsight gets you *fired*. I'd much rather be on the left side of that equation.

LESSON #60: BAD NEWS LIGHTSPEED APPROACH

One of the management rules that I've created for anyone who is on my direct report team is that *bad news must travel faster than good news*.

I call this the *bad news lightspeed approach*.

Let's face it. Everyone loves to deliver good news to their boss. Just won a big account? Just hit your sales milestone for the month? Just got a flattering note from a customer? Who doesn't like to do an all-out sprint to the boss' office to share great news with them!? I know I always have.

Bad news, on the other hand, now that's a totally different story.

In the workplace, bad news tends to be taboo. Nobody wants to see it and nobody wants to touch it. Nobody wants to talk about or hear about it. Well, guess what? That doesn't make it go away!

Bad news is like a carton of milk on its expiration date. If you drink it that day, you'll be safe, but the longer you keep it around, the more it will stink and the more it will corrode everything around it.

As a CEO, this has presented an extra difficult challenge to me, because nobody wants to be the one to deliver bad news to the CEO. Everyone views his or her job as one where they need to appease, placate and impress you. In my experience, the best thing you can do, not just if you're a CEO but if you're a manager of any kind, is to flip this notion upside down.

You need to create a culture where bad news is encouraged and welcomed, and that demands bad news is delivered in real time. As I tell my direct reports, bad news must travel at the speed of light.

By this point, my direct reports have been conditioned to bring me bad news immediately. This way, we can sit down, review and troubleshoot the bad news together. My direct reports pass this same rule on down to their direct reports and so on throughout our organization, all the way down to our entry-level employees.

The concept is pretty simple: The faster you learn about bad news, the faster you can treat it and find a solution. You can't fix it if you don't know about it!

The key to all this is, you need to have the right reporting relationship with your subordinates and you need to trust your subordinates to use discretion about what bad news to bring to your attention. If you're talking about the water cooler temperature being a few degrees lower than normal, it's probably not worth bringing to the boss' desk. Emergency client or employee issues? Now, that's a different story.

There needs to be mutual respect, trust and a desire to problem solve that unites both you and your subordinate. The *bad news lightspeed approach* requires mutual commitment and synergy on the part of both the subordinate and you as the manager. You need to trust your subordinates to use proper discretion about what bad news makes it to your desk, and trust that they will deliver it to you immediately. Your subordinates need to trust that you will internalize the problem and join with them to make a team decision. If they are fearful about delivering bad news to you, that is a toxic situation that will lead to a disastrous end to your relationship with your subordinates.

When it comes to bad news, it doesn't need to just travel fast — it needs to travel at the speed of light!

LESSON #61: SHORT-TERM EARNINGS VS. LONG-TERM RETURNS

Although I don't run a public company, which comes with the pressures of shareholder returns, regulatory filings and earnings calls, I still feel many of the stresses and anxieties that come with quarterly earnings. This is because, as the sole shareholder of our company, quarterly earnings hit me where it hurts the most, in the wallet!

We have been in business for more than 40 quarters. That's 10 years' worth of scrutinizing quarterly returns, P&Ls and earnings statements. Naturally, my ideology on quarterly earnings has changed, and I'd like to think I've learned quite a bit and matured over the years. For many years, I lived and died according to our quarterly earnings. If we had a high-performing quarter, I would rejoice. If we had a low-performing quarter, I would panic.

In the third quarter of 2016, we had adjusted earnings of more than $500,000. It was the first time we hit this milestone and I felt like I was on top of the world. In the first quarter of 2019, meanwhile, we had adjusted earnings that were a fraction of this amount, despite having top-line revenue that was considerably higher. I was panicked and stressed out, and I was convinced we were going out of business. I laugh at how ridiculous that seems now, but as my wife can verify, I was pretty miserable to be around during that time.

The only reason I bring this up is because these events have helped to shape my outlook toward quarterly earnings. It took me many years to arrive at this conclusion, but I no longer put much stock in them.

The truth is that no matter how we performed over the course of any given quarter, I was losing sight of the big picture. I was too focused on short-term earnings, which was inhibiting my ability to think long-term and to act as the best long-term growth agent for our business. This has been a painful lesson for me to learn. I believe if I had been less concerned with quarterly earnings and more concerned with long-term growth, our business would likely be two to three times our current size right now.

Quarterly earnings might give you *short-term gains*, but truly great *returns* for businesses are built over the long-term.

Earnings over a longer period (a given year, for example, or across multiple years) are a far more significant reflection of the health and upside of a business. Three months is far too short a window of time to draw any meaningful conclusions about the financial status, potential or long-term viability of any business. There are too many variables that can affect a business over a quarter. Conditions in the economic climate, the seasonality of a business, the ebbs and flows of a vertical industry in which a business has high client concentration and many factors can artificially depress or inflate earnings over a given quarter.

Additionally, it's too easy for slick executives and financial professionals to manipulate quarterly earnings by way of creative accounting methods or recognizing sales cycles in opportunistic ways.

If you're operating a privately held business without the pressures of a board, shareholders or governance requirements, you should take full advantage of this. Keep a bogie in place, either a profit margin or an absolute dollar amount of earnings you don't want to dip below. As long as you're operating within that bogie, you should be less concerned with your earnings over a given quarter, and more concerned with how you're setting the business up over the long term. Rather than obsess over quarterly earnings, create a quarterly vision scorecard or some other tool you can use to evaluate your performance against your long-term plans for growth.

Quarterly earnings are great for short-term gain and bragging rights to your friends, but truly great returns are generated by businesses that prioritize long-term vision.

LESSON #62: ENTER THE LION'S DEN

As proof that you're always learning new lessons in your career, here's one I didn't learn until I was 37.

Leaving a job or leaving certain people in your career can be tumultuous at times, but I learned something very important from one of our employees about confronting those feelings of awkwardness and discomfort.

Toward the end of 2019, we were pitching business to one of the largest publicly traded cybersecurity companies in the world. We had previously represented this company for many years, taking it from a small start-up to a $200 million acquisition, then taking it public on a leading stock exchange. This turned out to be one of our most successful case studies, and contributed significantly to our ability to scale over the years. As a result of the account, we won several industry awards, got invited to larger client pitches, and handled assignments for many clients that would go on to get acquired and file for public listings on the New York Stock Exchange, NASDAQ and other exchanges.

Following a successful partnership that lasted for many years, this client decided to suspend services with our firm upon the departure of its Chief Marketing Officer in 2018. The CMO had hired us and had served as a champion of ours for a long time. The CMO was a key executive who played an important role in the client's success, masterminding its demand generation, revenue and marketing efforts. But after the company was acquired in 2018, the CMO left, relocating to Tel-Aviv.

The CMO's departure was tumultuous and was an unfortunate end to an otherwise successful run that saw many people make a lot of money and accomplish great things that served to disrupt the cybersecurity industry. Things didn't end well between the CMO and some members of the management team, and the CMO never stepped foot into their offices after he left.

By the time the client called on us to pitch its business again in 2020, the CMO had begun working for our company. I had hired him the previous year in a consulting capacity as we were scaling our business and investing heavily in sales and marketing.

When we got invited to pitch the business, you can imagine how awkward and uncomfortable it was, particularly for the former CMO. The client had been an enigma in his career for many years. On the one hand, it represented a very successful chapter in his career. On the other, it represented a painful and unfortunate chapter that came with regret.

Heading into the client's office would be like entering a *lion's den* in many ways for this person, so I gave him the option of sitting out the pitch. I knew it would be uncomfortable for him, and I wasn't sure how the client's management team would respond to seeing him either. But he wanted to confront the situation head-on, choosing to not only to *join* the pitch meeting but to *lead* it.

In the end, we ended up winning the pitch, and the client became another successful case study for us in the second chapter of our relationship. The former CMO's return was well received by everyone at the company. Employees who hadn't seen him in years came up to hug him and shared great memories of him. Clearly, they wanted to put the past behind them just as much as he did.

This taught me a valuable lesson about confronting fears in the workplace, particularly when dealing with people. We all have our own *lion's den* when it comes to people in our careers, relationships that went south and that we have regrets over.

If it were me, I'm not sure I would've had the courage and strength that the former CMO had. I think I would've chickened out and done everything I could to avoid entering the *lion's den*.

The way he handled himself in the client pitch taught me to confront those fears head-on, to let bygones be bygones, and to enter the *lion's den* with enthusiasm and with a positive spirit.

At 37, I learned an important lesson. Even though it can be uncomfortable, don't avoid the *lion's den* when it comes to people. Enter the *lion's den* and don't look back.

LESSON #63: ISLANDS ARE FOR MARGARITAS, NOT FOR MANAGEMENT

With few exceptions, the "island" approach to management has failed me miserably whenever I've tried it out.

When you have an idealistic approach to management as I do, you tend to come up with reasons to convince yourself why someone *can* work out in a different role rather than rationalizing to yourself why they're *not* working out in their current role. This leads you to consider creating new positions or finding new places within your organization that don't currently exist and sometimes defy logic, just to retain an employee.

Anytime I've said to myself "this could work out in the long-run," it has always failed me before it's gotten to the point where I could even make the long-term evaluation.

Oftentimes I've thought to myself, perhaps this person is not working out in his current role, but if I created another position for him or shuffled around our org chart to carve out a new place for him, he'd work out just fine.

This is what I refer to as the "island" approach to management.

With the "island" approach, you identify the strengths in somebody who is not working out in his current role and *create* a new position as a response (i.e., his own "island"). Even though this is rooted in a good place, it has rarely worked out in my experience.

There's a difference between managing to someone's strengths and *creating* new roles for them that don't currently exist. Managing to one's strengths by fitting them into a better role that *already exists* on your team is a good quality in a manager.

I've tried out the "island" approach at least a dozen times, and it has resulted in a failed outcome each time.

For example, I've created new functions prematurely, based on speculation but not based on revenue demand. I've been so gaga after meeting a candidate that I felt the need to carve out a new role for the person because I felt it would fit into our future needs rather than our present needs. I've created special positions for people in order to separate them from others in the organization with whom they didn't get along.

The last example has resulted in the worst outcomes possible because it has sent a terrible message to the rest of the employees in the company:

"If you don't get along with your peers, don't worry about it, the company will create a new role for you!" That is an awful message to send your employees, and anytime I've done it, it has led to destructive outcomes.

The "island" approach is tricky. On the one hand, it shows that you have admirable vision, but on the other, it demonstrates poor discipline and a lack of pragmatism. If you have a uniquely skilled performer — someone who is not doing an adequate job in his or her current role but possesses a unique skill for which you feel you should create a new role — it demonstrates that you have vision and belief in the person's abilities. However, it also demonstrates that you cannot manage based on the current realities of your business and the present needs of your team.

Whenever I've made a decision to go with the "island" approach, the consequences have been severe. It has been disruptive to other areas of our business, and it has negatively impacted our service levels, investment allocation, employee retention and team morale. It's also been a painful lesson I've had to learn over and over again. You'd think I would have learned to avoid the "island" approach by now, but that hasn't been the case. Too many times, I've turned a blind eye to pragmatism and reality and yielded to my idealistic instinct by making the decision to create a brand-new position for someone who was underperforming in his or her current role.

As a manager, you really need to take a step back and assess the true needs of your team and the short-term demand in your business. If there is true need for a new position and it fits logically into your near-term needs, then it should be strongly considered. However, if you're creating a new role based on the *person*, not on the *needs* of the business, that's a decision that will usually backfire.

This is the "island" approach to management, and I wouldn't recommend it. Take it from someone who has learned this over and over again.

Islands are meant for *margaritas*, not for management.

LESSON #64: GOOD PEOPLE LEAD YOU TO GREAT PLACES

When I was just starting out in my career, I was blinded by the same things as so many recent college grads — what my salary would be, where my office would be, what types of clients I would work with. I *had* to keep up with the Joneses, I couldn't *possibly* tolerate making less money than my friends, and I absolutely *needed* to work at a company which had some sizzle. I made most of my early career decisions based on these factors.

In some cases, I left behind great people and great opportunities for 10, 15, even 20 percent salary increases. If I had to do it all over again, I would have taken the same factors into account to *support* my decision, but I would have looked at a completely different variable to *make* my decision: the *people*.

When I was in my early 20s, I jumped at the opportunity to make an $80,000 annual salary. While I did realize that I was getting a significant salary increase from my previous job, what I didn't realize that that I was leaving behind great people and great upside to do it. The people with whom I had previously worked were phenomenal. I trusted them, I respected them, and they supported me as I was finding my footing, as my career was just getting underway.

I jumped at the opportunity, however, because I saw $80,000 as life-changing money. The truth is, it felt like it at the time. What I found out quickly was that I was miserable, I was no longer surrounded by people who supported me in the workplace, and that $80,000 salary suddenly didn't seem so big anymore.

Other than having bragging rights over most of my friends who weren't making as much as I was, the paycheck was meaningless, it had no long-term impact on my career, and it made me realize how good I had it in my other job. As the years go by, the numbers don't seem as big, and bragging rights do absolutely nothing for you other than provide a shallow stroke to your fragile ego.

This turned out to be a great lesson for me after I started our business. It showed me the value of great people, which then turned out to be a guiding principle I've taken with me as I've built our company.

Good people will lead you to *great* places. I've found this to be true both in running a business and earlier in my career.

After I started our business, I realized that this principle rang truer than ever before. I've been very fortunate to have been surrounded by some great people over the course of the past decade. I've found that the better the people I've been surrounded by, the better the places and the opportunities in front of me.

Good people — people I can trust, people who support and challenge me — have led me to the biggest opportunities of my career. As I look back at the decade since we started our business, every big opportunity, whether it's been a huge account or a life-changing financial event, has been generated by people, not by money. We've always experienced our best business outcomes whenever we've had the best people. That tells you all you need to know.

Salary and other factors that go into your decision about where to work all have a tangible value attached to them, but people have an *intangible* value. They bring a depth and substance to your career that a paycheck can't provide.

When you're first starting out in your career, make sure your paycheck provides you with enough to pay your bills and live a reasonably comfortable life, but never let money be the deciding factor in where you work.

Good people lead you to *great* places. This has turned out to be one of the most valuable lessons I could ever learn in my career.

LESSON #65: THE "SCUSE" METHOD FOR CLOSING SALES

I've never had any formal sales training, but since starting our business I've learned my fair share of lessons about effective and ineffective sales tactics. After these years in the trenches, I've developed something called the "SCUSE" method and have found it to be a reliable go-to formula whenever I want to close a sale.

In 2013, I started making a concerted effort to study and analyze trends and patterns with sales prospects that I came across. I spent the next 24 months recording all sorts of data for each prospect, then studied the commonalities in deals I won and deals I lost. Through this exercise I discovered that 95 percent of the deals I had won included an effective display of each of the following steps:

Smart. I did something at some point in the sales process to show the prospect I was intelligent — demonstrating critical thinking skills, for example. I shared smart ideas or recommendations, insights on the competitive market or consultative advice that caused the prospect to see that I was more than just an empty suit.

Customized. I did something throughout the sales process to make the prospect feel like he was getting a customized and personalized experience from me. I studied his background, found out where he went to school, learned what his hobbies and other interests were, then shared information that clearly demonstrated I'd gone the extra mile to know who he really was.

Urgency. There was a level of urgency that I stressed in every one of the closed prospects. As I studied this one more closely, I discovered that this was a fine line. I displayed great urgency but was never desperate. As a result, the prospect understood that he was a top priority of mine and that I was enthusiastic about winning the business, yet never felt like I was desperate to win it.

Speed. I was fast, fast, fast. All of my responses to the prospect were in real time. I got back to him immediately. I shared deliverables with him before he had a chance to remind me. Any requests were met with a lightning-quick turnaround. I was clearly the fastest of all the service providers the prospect was considering.

Efficiency. I was efficient with my time on all of the deals that I won. I didn't waste any time or overthink things. I didn't get swallowed alive in any of the minutiae, and most of the time I spent on each deal was facing the prospect as opposed to behind the scenes. I knew when to apply pressure, I knew when to lay off, and knew when to go in for the close.

I followed each of these steps for 95 percent of the deals that I closed. Meanwhile, for 98 percent of the deals that I lost, I didn't follow this method. The statistics were startling to me.

With this analysis, the "SCUSE" method was born. From that point forward, I've adopted the "SCUSE" method in all of my efforts to manage relationships with sales prospects along the path to closing.

Since implementing the "SCUSE" method, our close rates on qualified prospects have increased by 20 percent, the average deal value has increased by 40 percent, and the average length of our sales cycles has decreased by 15 days. Not only has the "SCUSE" method made me a more effective closer, it's also helped to compress time, showing prospects a level of intelligence and urgency during the sales process that convinces them to accelerate their buying decisions.

I've also trained everyone on our sales team to follow this process. In time, I've learned that the steps of the "SCUSE" method are also transferrable to other functions and departments. The method has served our account management team well in its efforts to build, nurture and retain relationships with existing clients. The method has helped our talent development team in its efforts to recruit new talent to our company.

If you're in sales and looking to improve your success rate, give the "SCUSE" method a shot.

Even if you're not in sales, you should try it out. There are no *excuses*. There's only the *"SCUSE"* method, and it works!

LESSON #66: BE THE CEO OF YOUR DEPARTMENT

Every Monday morning, I meet with my direct reports, bright and early at 8 o'clock. It has become an important part of our operation that enables us to review, prioritize and align on goals before the week begins.

This has become our management team's version of a war room preparation session before the battle begins. The meetings include me and the heads of our sales, service, operations and finance departments. Breakfast is served, reports are spread across the boardroom table, and an agenda is on display on the TV screen, with three words in bright letters:

Know your department.

The words are so simple, yet I've found that only a small minority of people truly know their departments. Over time, I've learned that not only should you *know* your department, you should become the *CEO* of your department.

CEO of your department is a mindset and commitment to studying and preparing so that nobody knows more about your department or role within the organization than you do. This should begin as soon as you start your career, not when you move into a manager role.

Since starting our business, I've observed that those who get promoted the fastest and most frequently are those who have a *CEO of your department* mindset. Meanwhile, the ones who remain stagnant in their current roles for the longest periods of time are the ones who lack this mindset.

I remember meeting the CEO of a larger, competing public relations firm at an industry event in 2012. After talking to her about her role within her business, it was evident that she knew much more about her role as CEO of her company than I did as CEO of mine. It was an embarrassing experience frankly.

She was able to recite chapter and verse about industry benchmarks and actual company performance compared to historical trends, among other things that I simply had no idea about. She was clearly someone who had the *CEO of your department* mindset, while I didn't have anything close to it at the time. From that day forward, I've always made sure that *nobody* knew more about my department or role than I do, and I've held my direct reports to the same standard.

My direct reports are great examples of the *CEO of your department* mindset. During those Monday morning meetings, I'll watch as our Chief Operating Officer takes us to school on our service operation, reciting client attrition trends by industry, customer service rankings and satisfaction scores, and discussing trends and patterns within our client portfolio that nobody else can see. I'll observe as our Chief Financial Officer takes a deep dive into our finance function, analyzing spend patterns by department, sharing insights on expenditure by level, and predicting future revenue scenarios based on historical patterns. The same is true of our heads of sales and operations. Each knows his or her own department like nobody's business. They have literally become the CEOs of their departments.

While *CEO of your department* might seem like an advanced concept reserved only for senior managers, that is the furthest thing from the truth. The earlier in your career that you adopt this mindset, the sooner you will see your career accelerate at a faster and more rewarding pace than your peer set.

If you're in an entry-level role where your primary duties are administrative in nature, you should still adopt the *CEO of your department* approach to your position. You should study administrative trends that have worked well for others, conduct timing analyses to improve your speed on deliverables, and spend time researching what other professionals in your same role, both inside and outside your industry, are doing. This will help you master your craft, and most importantly it will lead you to knowing your department better than anybody else. You should never be outworked or outstudied by anyone in your peer set.

In time, you will find that your work product is faster, more efficient and of higher quality than others in your peer set. In all likelihood, you'll leave the administrative job in the dust and get promoted ahead of your peers.

The same can be said no matter which level you are in your organization. Whether it's entry level or senior management, revenue generating or non-revenue generating, service or support, everyone can be the *CEO of their department.* It's a mindset and commitment that requires time, effort and preparation, but one that always pays off in the end.

Study your department. *Know* your department. Become the *CEO of your department.*

LESSON #67: DON'T BE LATE

I am not a stickler for many things, but tardiness is definitely one of them.

I've softened my approach to management in many ways over the years, but I still like to show up to everything on time, and I expect the same from those who are on my team. I am rarely late for meetings. In fact, I prefer to show up at least 15 minutes early to most meetings. With modern technology, there is no reason to be late for anything nowadays. Traffic reports, commuting alternatives and transit updates are all available in the palm of your hands. All you need is a warm body, and technology can do all the rest to ensure you show up on time.

Back in 2014, I put in place a rule at our company called the "Belichick Rule." It was modeled after football coach Bill Belichick, who would send players home if they showed up late to practice. It wasn't done with disrespectful intentions. I instituted it because I wanted to show that it was important to show up on time, and that there would be no special treatment for anyone. If you showed up late to work — whether it was by 5 minutes or 5 hours — it didn't matter. You were asked to take the day as personal time off (PTO). You left the office with your dignity before you came back the next day.

Looking back at it, creating the "Belichick Rule" was probably a poor decision of mine, which was the reason I suspended it a year later. It was too extreme, there was no room for discretion, and it was an unnecessary measure that I took to prove a point. It was a failed experiment, and one of the decisions that I regret when I look back on how I managed people over the years.

However, even though the "Belichick Rule" was a failed experiment, the fact remains, you should *always* show up on time. Simply put, time is money in the workplace, and if you're showing up late, it means that you're impacting your company with lost productivity and opportunity costs.

I believe timeliness shows a respect for others in the workplace, and is usually connected to other qualities that translate to success in high-stakes parts of the job such as multitasking, handling high-pressure situations, meeting deadline requirements and optimizing time efficiencies.

In fairness, this is a generalization. Some of the most successful people I've come across have been laissez-faire in their approach to timeliness, and some of the least successful people I've come across have never showed up late to one meeting. However, generally speaking, the ones who show up on time usually display winning qualities in other aspects of their jobs.

Yours truly learned this lesson the hard way in 2016. I was enroute to a highly lucrative client pitch meeting and completely misread the address of the prospect's office. I showed up at Union Square, when the prospect's office was actually around *Herald* Square, 20 blocks or so from where I was. I notified the prospect that I was running late and hopped on the next subway uptown.

However, by the time I arrived, the damage had already been done. It turned out that the CEO of the company whose business we were pitching was just as much of a stickler for tardiness as I was. He allowed our team to continue with the pitch meeting, but every 10 minutes or so he reminded me how rude I was to have shown up late and how difficult it would be for his company to work with a firm that didn't respect time and deadline requirements.

Even though he was a real jerk about it, his point was valid. Of course, we lost the prospect's account, and it ended up costing us a $250,000 annual contract. Even though it was an honest mistake that caused me to show up late to the meeting, it didn't matter to the prospect. The outcome was the same, and the prospect didn't really care that I was never late to other meetings. All he cared about was that I was late to *his* meeting.

I've never been late to a meeting since that day, and I've made a vow to never let it happen again.

I no longer overmanage to prove a point or implement extremely harsh rules like the "Belichick Rule" to ensure timeliness, but the message remains just as important as it ever has: Don't be late.

LESSON #68: CONFLICT RESOLUTION 101: FIGHT OR FOLLOW-UP?

Conflict is unavoidable in a management relationship. Whenever you work with someone as closely and intimately as your boss or subordinate, you're going to encounter conflict. Anytime you put the number of hours into a relationship that a manager and subordinate put into working with each other, the relationship is going to be tested time and time again in the face of conflict.

How that conflict is handled and ultimately resolved is usually a good sign of the health and stability of the relationship between a manager and their subordinate.

One thing I've learned over the years is that all managers should develop a conflict resolution policy — something that clearly lays out the manager's preferred process and philosophy for troubleshooting conflict whenever it arises in his or her working relationship with subordinates.

Whenever new people join my direct report team, I share my conflict resolution policy with them on their first day on the job. This way, they immediately understand how to approach things whenever conflict inevitably rears its ugly head in our working relationship.

My conflict resolution policy is pretty straightforward:

Fight or follow-up.

This is how I prefer to resolve conflict with people who work alongside me.

The choice is the subordinate's, not mine. We have two options to resolve a conflict in our working relationship: We can either fight it out right there on the spot or we can sleep on it and have a follow-up the next day. I let my subordinates choose which one they want, so they feel empowered to make the decision rather than feeling like I'm forcing the decision on them. However, once the decision is made, we must resolve our issue right there. I don't like any animosity or bad blood to linger longer than it needs to, so once the subordinate makes the choice to fight or follow up, the rule is that we have to resolve our conflict in the moment.

If they choose the "fight" option, we have to resolve the conflict in real time, always behind closed doors. It can often get ugly (hence the word "fight"), with emotions running high and usually with some nasty comments exchanged. This typically happens because the wound from the conflict is so fresh in the "fight" option. If they choose the "fight" option, we're making a concerted decision to find a resolution right there on the spot, no matter how ugly it gets. We're not allowed to leave the room until we come to a resolution that both parties are content with and our working relationship is back on healthy footing.

If they choose the "follow-up" option, we sleep on the conflict and come back to it the next day. This gives both parties a chance to calm down and think about potential resolutions with a clear head. I've found that this option is most effective for larger and more complex conflicts where a bit of time and distance are best served to help troubleshoot the issue. The same rule applies as it does with the "fight" option. Once we follow up the next day, the conflict must be resolved in the moment, leaving nothing to linger and making sure that we are both content with the resolution. When subordinates choose the "follow-up" option, I prefer to use a neutral location the next day rather than meet in the office. This way, there is a fresh location with no leftover remnants from the original conflict. It gives us a chance to resolve the conflict from a clean slate and with a completely clear and impartial approach.

The fight or follow-up policy has been very effective for me in my continued efforts to establish healthier relationships with my subordinates and to become a better manager. It has helped to ensure that we have a transparent, expedient and productive way to resolve conflicts together whenever they arise.

Fight or follow-up doesn't work for everyone, however. It all comes down to the people and personalities involved. Some manager-subordinate relationships would have disastrous endings if they implemented such a policy. The important thing is not what your policy is — it's that you have a policy in the first place, and that you're open with your subordinates on how you prefer to approach conflict whenever it inevitably tests your working relationships.

Conflict resolution 101. What's your policy? You'd better have one.

LESSON #69: BE THERE FOR YOUR TEAMMATES

In 2006, I was recruited by a New York-based public relations firm to manage a team of people in one of its practice areas. It was the first time I was tasked with managing a group of people. I tried my best to hide it, but the truth is that I was intimidated when I first took the job, mainly because the people I was managing were considerably older and more experienced than I was. I was 23 years old and most of my co-workers were in their late 20s and early 30s.

Although I was reluctant, I accepted the challenge and worked longer hours and put in extra effort to get to know the people I was managing and show them I was capable of doing the job. Within the first few months, things were going remarkably smoothly. I quickly learned to love the management role, our practice area was growing rapidly, and my subordinates seemed to take a liking to me and to my leadership style, which was more personal, energetic and hands-on than they were used to.

Then I learned a big lesson that I haven't forgotten since. A few months into the role, one of my subordinates lost his father unexpectedly. Over the few months since we had started working together, he and I had developed a strong relationship and mutual respect for each other. We came from similar backgrounds and developed a unique bond in the workplace.

Even though the subordinate was a few years older than I was, he looked up to me in many ways, as if I were a brother figure. But when it was time for his father's funeral, I didn't show up. Frankly, I didn't have any reason not to go. I was single at the time, living in Brooklyn without any family obligations. The funeral was a few short blocks from my apartment and I could have easily cut out of work early to attend. But I didn't, and it was a big regret that taught me an important lesson.

While the subordinate never told me so, I could sense he was disappointed. Our relationship was never the same after that. I subsequently left to join another firm, and we lost touch.

I internalized this incident a lot and was really disappointed in myself. I should've known better. Forget about it being the right thing to do professionally — showing up to the funeral would've been the right thing to do as a human being, and I didn't do it. It wasn't how I was raised, and I felt really terrible about the whole thing.

This was a big lesson for me. When I started our business a few years later, I made a promise to myself that I would always try to be there for our employees whenever they went through life events such as weddings, the births of their children and the deaths of loved ones. I'm sure I don't have a perfect track record, but it's important to me and I've always made my best effort to show my support.

Over the years, my wife would get frustrated at times, and understandably so. At times I would miss my own family's events in order to attend those of our employees. However, it is important to me that I show support, and I'm glad I've done so through the years. It has brought a much greater sense of purpose and meaning to my career. I remember the feeling of regret and disappointment from missing that funeral years ago, and I don't want to feel like that again.

What kind of leader would I be and what kind of example would I set for others if I only showed support during work moments but was a no-show during their life moments? Their life moments were obviously more important to them than anything they would go through in the office.

I've shared many meaningful moments with our employees in the office over the past decade, but the ones that I'm most proud of were the ones that we've shared outside the office. I think these moments have had the most impact on me and on them, and they've resulted in us forming strong relationships that were built on mutual respect.

Obviously, life, family and geographic obstacles have prevented me from attending every one of our employees' life events, but I do my best to attend as many as I can. For the ones that I can't attend, I try to be present and show support in other ways.

Be there for your teammates. Not because it's the right thing to do for *work*, but because it's the right thing to do for *them*. This was an important lesson I learned back in 2006, and I haven't forgotten it since.

LESSON #70: DISCIPLINE IS SEXY

Discipline does not get the acclaim that "vision," "disruption" and other, sexier business buzzwords get, but in my experience it's every bit as important to building a successful business. I'm on a mission to turn "discipline" into a sexy word in business nomenclature.

Yes, *discipline is sexy*. Let me tell you why.

One of the advantages of running a client services business is that you get exposure to all sorts of companies and you get a line of sight into how each of them operates. In my experience, the biggest difference between businesses that achieve sustainable, long-term success and those that have short periods of success but struggle over the long term is their operating disciplines.

Entrepreneurs tend to be passionate and inventive product masters, but oftentimes they lose sight of the importance of operating discipline along the way. Passion and invention will give you the fuel you need to *start* your business, but operating discipline will give you the fuel you need to *stay* in business. I've always tried to operate our business as if we were two to three times our size at each step of the way.

When we were a $1 million business and lacked a dedicated finance function, I would sit down at my father's kitchen table once per month and review profit and loss statements, tax accrual progress trackers and sales reports. It was small and intimate, but things like this demonstrated that we had the operating discipline of a $3 million business even though we were much smaller.

When we were a $5 million business with dedicated functions, we implemented processes that much larger organizations had in place — quarterly business reviews, for example — and we adopted more advanced accounting methods. It was considerably more advanced than our size at the time, but it demonstrated that we were capable of operating a business that was $15 million in revenue.

We've followed this rule even through today. We continue to run our operation with a business discipline and rigor that much larger operations have in place. This has helped to prepare us for the next level of scale at every stage, as we've always been operating as if we were at the next level.

I've been an avid student of larger companies from the very first day I opened our business. I've always listened to podcasts, read books and watched interviews featuring executives who run larger companies to pick up pointers and get a sense for their operating disciplines. I've noticed that most of them have a rigor and repetition that is admirable, and I've tried to adopt many of their practices into our own business.

For example, after listening to an interview with a Cargill executive about the company's monthly financial checkpoint sessions, we implemented a monthly financial review session, complete with financial packages that analyze cash flow and balance sheet movements, financial performance versus key performance indicators (KPIs), and forecast and budget refreshers just like the Cargill executive had explained.

After listening to a Harvard Business Review podcast on human resource discipline, we created recurring human resource checkpoint sessions, where we do a rigorous review of our healthcare and 401(k) offerings, comparative analysis of our benefits versus the competition and cost-benefit analysis of our suite of benefits.

After watching a TED Talk about recruiting analytics, we created a process where we assess the demands of the employment market, the competitiveness of our compensation packages, and the adequacy of our org chart. We do this across the board, within every department and every aspect of our business.

Now *that* is discipline.

It might seem boring to you, but it's *sexy* to me. And it's been just as much a contributor to our growth and success over time as anything else.

Any business can experience short-term flashes of success. However, it's very difficult, almost impossible, for a business to experience long-term success over a sustainable period of time without demonstrating strong operating discipline backed by rigor and repetition. Proper checks and balances, regular reviews of department analytics and accountability checkpoints for performance versus KPIs all demonstrate strong operating discipline. These are all fundamental parts of scaling a business over a sustained period of time.

I'm perfectly fine if someone says my vision, innovation and disruption leave a lot to be desired. Just don't call me a poorly disciplined business operator. That I'll never be.

I'll always be disciplined. Now that is *sexy* to me.

LESSON #71: INCREMENTALISM IS SEXIER

Here's another word that doesn't get the credit it deserves in business.

Incrementalism.

Now, that's even *sexier* than discipline!

No success in business or in your career can come without incrementalism — the act of improving in small but meaningful doses over a long period of time. Any modicum of success we've achieved as a company over the past decade has been the result of incrementalism.

In 2010, we were an unproven start-up with some gaping holes. In 2011, we plugged a few of those holes and became a proven start-up with some leftover holes that still needed to be plugged.

In 2012, we plugged those leftover holes, and we became a good business.

In 2013, we plugged a few more holes and we became a *really* good business. We kept doing this year after year, and here we are a decade later, stronger than we've ever been.

We are a *great* business today because of the annual improvements that we've made. Our business is nothing more than the manifestation of a decade's worth of incremental improvements and plugging small holes time after time. Great companies and great careers are built over time by making incremental improvements at every checkpoint. I've seen this manifest itself in great talent, as well.

Our Executive Vice President of Talent Development, Nina Velasquez, is a great example of someone whose success is the biproduct of incrementalism. Nina has been with our company for eight years, nearly 80 percent of our entire existence. She started as a mid-level client services director in 2012. She was great at her craft back then, which was in a client-side public relations service capacity. However, in order to grow to the next level, she kept making small improvements to work on other parts of her game. She improved by adding new skills such as strategy, people management and business acumen to her repertoire. She did this repeatedly, year after year, until she eventually rose to become a Vice President, Senior Vice President and then Executive Vice President.

Nina now runs our talent department, and does a terrific job overseeing our recruiting and professional development efforts. She has brought the best talent in our industry through our doors, and helped retain and prepare our staff for the next levels of their career growth. Nina's role today is completely different from the client services role that she inherited when she began working for us eight years ago. It requires a completely different skillset. She was able to successfully transform and reinvent her career over a long period of time because she made small, incremental improvements in short spurts on a consistent basis and without exception.

The same thing can be said of many other highly successful people I've encountered through the years. My Chief of Staff John Hannaway began working for us five years ago in a specifically defined administrative role with limited upside earnings potential. Five years later, he's operating as a C-suite executive, wearing many hats and earning 50 percent more than he earned when he first started. This is the result of incrementalism.

All of these people are successful because they made commitments to plug small holes over a long period of time without exception. They are great examples of incrementalism in action. Oftentimes in your career, you feel the need to redefine yourself overnight. You're trying to move from the role you're in to the one you want in a matter of seconds. Rather than trying to get there overnight, you should focus on improving yourself in small doses on a consistent basis. If you commit to doing this for a long period of time, that's when you'll realize the benefit and see your career take shape in ways that you never imagined.

Discipline might be sexy, but incrementalism is *sexier*. I've seen it time and time again in the most successful people that I know.

LESSON #72: ACCOUNTABILITY IS THE SEXIEST

If discipline is sexy and incrementalism is sexier, another word is the *sexiest* when it comes to your career journey:

Accountability.

In time, I've learned that accountability is what truly separates average teammates from great teammates in the workplace. Ultimately, you are accountable for every decision that you make in your career.

Don't like the place where you're currently working? You're accountable for staying there.

Don't respect the boss that you're working for? You're accountable for choosing to work for that person.

Frustrated by that failed client outcome? You're probably accountable in some way for the execution that led to it.

The hardest part about accountability in the workplace is that, as you rise higher up on the org chart, you become *more* accountable but *further* removed from many of the decisions that led to the outcomes.

Take my role as CEO, for example. We'll swing and miss on a recruiting candidate every so often (hey, it happens!). From time to time, we'll lose out on a client pitch that we really wanted to win. We'll misfire on a client project that we really needed to nail. Despite not making one of the decisions that led to these outcomes, I am accountable for all of them in some way. And guess what? I'm totally fine with it.

This is the blessing and the curse of being the boss. You're accountable for the outcomes even when you're not in the driver's seat on the decisions that led to them. It's tricky because it's your job to empower others to make decisions, but ultimately you need to feel comfortable being held accountable for the decisions they make.

The trick to all of this is that you must create a culture of top-down accountability. This usually comes down to hiring the right people and making sure the culture of accountability is understood by all. Everyone needs to understand that they are making decisions that will not just impact themselves but will ultimately trickle up the org chart if the decisions go wrong. The onus of accountability will fall on their boss, and then their boss' boss, all the way up to the CEO of the company. When this responsibility is understood and respected by all levels within the organization, that's when you have built a special team.

One of the things that I love about our company today is that we have achieved top-down accountability within our organization. This was a major challenge for our company in our formative years, but really started to change a few years ago when we began training and hiring stronger mid-level managers.

While accountability was always understood by our senior managers, our junior staff didn't quite understand the impact of their decisions on others when we were in our earlier years. Our mid-level managers were the ones who had a direct line to all levels of the organization, so their impact was felt from senior management to our entry-level workforce. They were the ones who became agents of change for accountability within our organization. They understood the culture of accountability and the impact that poor decisions would have on the managers above them. They took it very seriously and passed it down to the people they were managing. Before we knew it, there was a culture of top-down accountability, one where the entire organization knew that their decisions would have an impact on the managers above them if they went wrong. Once this happened, we started to scale quickly.

The culture of top down accountability has created a greater sense of pride, responsibility and maturity in the decision making across our entire company. As a result, we've seen our decision-making error rate drop dramatically, our standards for recruiting talent become higher, and our level of tolerance for poor performers, particularly for those with poor attitudes, drop to zero.

Of all of the catalysts for scale, I've found that a culture of top-down accountability has been the most impactful of them all. We scaled moderately when we had moderate accountability, but we scaled aggressively when we began having top-down accountability.

We became a *sexy* company once we understood the importance of discipline.

We became an even *sexier* company once we understood the role of incrementalism in the workplace.

But we became the *sexiest* company once we created a culture of accountability from the top down.

Accountability. Now *that's* the sexiest quality you could possess in your career.

LESSON #73: ALWAYS PAY IT FORWARD

The lesson about how I learned to always pay it forward in my career goes back half a century. Like most good things my career has produced, I have other people to thank for this lesson. It is a story of harmony and friendship that breaks through racial and socioeconomic barriers, and that captures the true essence of what it means to help each other out.

In the early 1970s, my mother was a first-year second grade schoolteacher on the south side of Mount Vernon, New York. The city was racially divided at that time, with the majority of the north side being working-class Irish and Italian families and the south side being predominantly black and Hispanic families. There was my mother, in her early 20s, the daughter of Italian immigrants, choosing to get her career kickstarted on the south side of Mount Vernon as one of the only white teachers in a school where over 90 percent of the students and teachers were black or Hispanic. That took a great deal of courage and self-confidence during this era.

In her class was a young black student named Dawn Short. Dawn immediately took a liking to my mother and looked up to her as a role model. All through elementary school, Dawn continued to visit my mother. The two stayed in touch for many years. Dawn would approach my mother for advice and for conversation, and she and my mother developed a close bond that would last for years to come.

Even though my mother never told me this, I'm convinced that Dawn helped her get adjusted to life as a teacher just as much as my mother helped Dawn develop into a confident and intelligent young woman. That is a beautiful lesson in itself.

Years later, Dawn would go on to achieve great things in her career. Eventually she rose to become one of the most powerful human resource executives at Sony BMG and one of the most successful female executives of a Fortune 500 company.

Fast-forward to 2005. Yours truly had just graduated from college and was in desperate need of a job. I searched far and wide, but couldn't get an offer anywhere. I went on job interview after job interview only to keep receiving template-style rejection letters.

After much lamenting to my mother, she decided to put in a call to Dawn. It didn't take much convincing at all. Being the selfless person that she is, Dawn arranged for me to interview with the marketing department at Sony BMG. Soon after, I got an offer, which I happily accepted. This became my first full-time job and marked the beginning of my career in marketing services. A year later, I parlayed the Sony BMG job into an agency job, and then a few years later I started my own company.

I have Dawn to thank for helping me get my start in business. She used to call me her little brother and she would look over me as if she were a big sister, which I desperately needed when I was working at Sony BMG, as I had just lost my older sister a year earlier. I'll never forget the many late-night calls I would get from Dawn to check on me and see how I was doing, or all the times she would swing by with a smile and put her arm around me when I needed one.

This is really a lesson in harmony and the importance of always paying it forward. My mother helped Dawn by serving as a maternal presence during her formative years, and Dawn paid it forward by helping me get my career started decades later. I've always tried to remember this lesson and to pay it forward myself whenever I've encountered a young person in his or her career who was in need of a favor.

We all have people in our careers who have paid it forward to us and have helped put us where we are today.

Thank you, Dawn, for being someone who paid it forward to me. You gave me my start in business and really are a big sister to me.

LESSON #74: YOU ARE NOT SELF-MADE

This is a difficult lesson for me to write about since I'm usually uncomfortable discussing financial achievements. However, it's a valuable lesson that I've learned, and for this reason alone I felt it was important to share it.

After I started our business, I got a taste of the financial trappings of success rather quickly. By our second year, we were already approaching $1 million in profits and I was able to provide my family with a very comfortable lifestyle. It was something that was completely new for me and my family, seeing as how less than five years earlier, I was an entry-level employee at Sony BMG making $30,000 a year.

Once I started seeing steady profits flow through the business, I set a goal of accumulating $1 million dollars in assets by the time I turned 30. Looking back on this now, it seems like such a vain and pretentious goal. As I've gotten deeper into my career, I no longer use financial milestones as goals for myself, but at that stage in my life and career this was an important goal and I desperately wanted to reach it.

Sure enough, the business kept growing and I reached my goal of having $1 million dollars by the time I was 30. By that point, I had paid off my mortgage in full, I had a nice nest egg, and I had met my goal of having a net worth of at least $1 million dollars by age 30. It was a great feeling of accomplishment at the time, and it was considerably further than anybody in my family had made it before at that age.

I was proud because I had accomplished all of this on my own, without taking any handouts or asking for any favors from anyone. I was *self-made*. Or so I thought.

As the years went by, our business kept growing.

By 2014, we had scaled considerably, and the profits kept coming in. I was invited to hear Ken Langone speak at Fordham University and quickly became a fan of his. I went on to read about him and listened closely to a lot of his ideology about business, management and success. Langone was a self-made billionaire, the son of blue-collar parents who had made it all the way to the pinnacle of American business. He was the co-founder of Home Depot, a legendary philanthropist and the lead donor of the NYU Langone hospital.

"I am not self-made!" Langone said in one interview I listened to.

How is it possible that he *is not self-made?* I thought to myself.

Here is a guy who is literally the definition of self-made — someone who rose from humble roots, didn't ask for any favors along the way, and ultimately turned himself into one of the most iconic examples of American business success of the past generation.

A few years later, Langone would delve deeper into the "self-made" topic in his book. He explained that was not self-made because he was the product of many hard-working people who helped him through the years. They might not have helped him financially, but they helped him with a resource that was far more valuable than money. They helped him with their *time*.

He wrote about all of the people who had given him their time and who had believed in him, people such as his parents, his wife, close friends and mentors. If it weren't for these people, Langone acknowledged, he would never have achieved the levels of success he did. For this reason, he argued, he was *not* self-made.

This was a big turning point in my career. Not only did I stop using financial milestones as goals for myself, but I also realized that I was not self-made.

I thought back over the years to the many people who had given me their time and who had believed in me — my parents, my wife, our early clients who took a chance on me, mentors who guided me, former employees who went to work for me when nobody else would, and peers in the industry who offered me advice and didn't charge me for it because they knew I had no money.

It dawned on me that these were the people who were responsible for my success over my first few years in business. I was the furthest thing from self-made. My success was nothing more than the product of great people who had given me the most generous gift of all, their *time*.

We often lose sight of the fact that success in our careers is typically the result of others as opposed to our own. *Nobody* is self-made. Even though this is an uncomfortable topic for me to write about, it is one of the most valuable lessons that I've learned over my first decade in business.

I owe a debt of gratitude to Ken Langone for teaching me this lesson through his words. More importantly, I owe an even bigger debt of gratitude to all the people who gave me their time and who believed in me over the past decade, and who showed me that, in fact, I am not self-made.

LESSON #75: CONTROL BUCKET 3

By 2012, our client base had grown considerably. It felt like every day we were either signing a new client or bidding farewell to an old one. As the CEO of our company, I found it to be increasingly challenging to keep up with all of the client movement. It was difficult for me keep pace with clients that were onboarding, and it was even more difficult for me to understand why clients were leaving. With this in mind, I started to study the patterns of all clients that departed over the next 12 months.

I spent the next year analyzing every client that had left our firm. Immediately following any departure, I would get on the phone with the client contact and have a one-on-one conversation regarding the decision to leave. Why were they leaving our firm? Was it something we did? Was there something wrong with our service? Was there a pricing concern? What was their customer service experience like? What was their impression of the cost-value relationship?

I genuinely wanted to get to the bottom of any client departure so I could understand the reason for leaving, and hopefully prevent it from happening again.

After a year of studying the patterns, the data was startling. I found that every single one of our client departures fit into one of three buckets: financial reasons, relationship reasons or service reasons. From this exercise, our "Bucket 3" philosophy was born.

Approximately one-third of the client departures could be put into "Bucket 1." These were clients that left for some financial-related reason. The reasons typically included their own lack of funding, forced budget cuts, financial performance problems, missed sales targets or excess spending in another department. They were forced to terminate their contracts with us for some type of financially motivated reason. I called these clients "Bucket 1's."

Another one-third of departures went into "Bucket 2." These were clients that left for a reason that was motivated by a change in the relationship. Typically, this meant that the client had hired an in-house resource to manage its relationship with our firm. In most cases, our previous day-to-day contact had left for another job and was replaced by someone who already had his or her own vendor relationships in place. This meant that we would be a casualty to a "Bucket 2" termination, and the client bid us adieu for relationship reasons.

Then, there was "Bucket 3." These were departures that were motivated by service reasons. These clients were dissatisfied with the service experience for one reason or another. The most common reasons for these terminations were missed KPIs, dissatisfaction with the strategic counsel or recommendations we delivered, lack of understanding the client's business, or the client's feeling that it would have a better service experience if it hired another firm.

When I first conducted this analysis, the numbers were mind-numbing. Out of all of the clients that terminated us over the previous 12 months, all of them could be put into one of these three buckets, with nearly an equal amount of terminations spread across each bucket.

Immediately after the analysis was complete, I called an impromptu staff meeting to present the data to our service employees. The message to the employees was simple: Control Bucket 3!

The first two buckets were clearly out of our control. We had virtually no control over the financial decisions of our clients, which ones would receive funding, which ones would hit their sales targets, and which ones would be forced to cut budgets. Likewise, we had no control over the relationship decisions of our clients, which ones would bring on new Chief Marketing Officers, which ones would fire our day-to-day contacts, and which of our client contacts would leave for greener pastures.

However, when it came to Bucket 3, we had full control over the outcomes. These were self-inflicted wounds that triggered the client terminations, and clearly were controllable mistakes that we made. From that point forward, we've had a zero-tolerance policy for Bucket 3 terminations. The concept is simple. While we can't control financial or relationship decisions, we can control our standards when it comes to service. As long as we controlled Bucket 3 terminations, we would be just fine.

Ever since then, we've implemented a rigorous Bucket 3 statistical analysis. Anytime a client leaves, we diagnose the reason for the termination and assign the client to one of the three buckets. Each month, we analyze our Bucket 3 terminations with a fine-tooth comb. We've never criticized or reprimanded a member of our service team for a Bucket 1 or Bucket 2 termination. But Bucket 3 terminations? That's the one we lose sleep over and examine with a microscope.

Our Bucket 3 statistics have dropped significantly since we first started doing this analysis. It's created a level of accountability and pride of authorship within our organization. Simply put, nobody wants to lose a Bucket 3 client.

If you're in a client-facing role, remember the "Buckets" philosophy. Control what's in your control. Control the Bucket 3's and everything else will be just fine.

LESSON #76: THE SOHO STROLL

This might sound like a story of confrontation and conflict, but read through to the end and you will see why it is one of the greatest lessons of triumph and character I've witnessed in my career.

This lesson was taught to me in 2016 by my future Chief of Staff John Hannaway, just after he had started working for our company as Vice President of Operations.

I have known John all my life. We grew up together, played Little League, worked at the same summer camp, attended ballgames and concerts together and went on road trips.

Whenever I need to have a serious work-related conversation with someone, I usually do it by taking a walk in SoHo, the downtown Manhattan neighborhood where we operate. I find the fresh air and change of scenery to be much less intimidating than the office for my subordinates and more conducive to confronting tough topics. Plus, we work in such a pristine neighborhood, removed from the hustle and bustle of midtown Manhattan, that I've found SoHo to be the perfect backdrop for serious talks.

In time, these walks came to be known by me and my direct reports as "SoHo strolls."

The stroll I took with John Hannaway in March 2016 was unlike any I had taken before, however. And no matter how pretty the backdrop, this would be an ugly one.

Before hiring him, I was very open with our staff about my personal relationship with John. I didn't want to hide it from them. I felt it was important that I disclosed that we were friends, and that the staff understood the working dynamic between me and John.

If you've ever worked with a friend or family member, you understand that it's not always an easy dynamic. Just like anything else, there are pros and cons. On the positive side, you get the benefit of working with someone you can trust, someone who you know will give you honest feedback. On the negative side, it's difficult to separate one's personal life from one's work life at times, and the difficult conversations that managers inevitably need to have with their subordinates threaten to impact your friendship.

This is what made this particular stroll such a difficult one for me. You see, John wasn't working out. He was working hard, but he simply wasn't getting the job done in his role, and it was hurting the company.

After leaving his previous job at a nonprofit, John was overwhelmed by the pace and the volume of responsibilities in his position with our company. He was asked to wear many hats, including human resources, finance and general office management. Consequently, other department heads and I were getting pulled into things that were taking time away from our jobs.

Here's a snippet of the feedback I gave John in his monthly performance report the Friday prior to our walk:

"John is hurting our company as a result of his inability to adjust to our pace and environment. I have serious concerns about his ability to perform his duties and am questioning whether we both made a mistake by recruiting him for this position. The impact to our company could be severe if he doesn't turn it around soon."

I didn't pull any punches. The following Monday morning, I walked over to his office and nodded toward the coat rack.

"Let's go for a walk and get some fresh air," I said to him. He knew what was coming.

As we walked down Mercer Street, I asked him how he felt he was performing. John has always been the consummate professional and operated with great integrity, so he had no problem owning up to his recent performance.

"I'm not getting the job done and I feel terrible about it," John said to me.

As we turned off Mercer Street onto Prince Street, I looked at him and began to respond.

"John, this is not going to be easy for me to say." I think he thought that he was going to get fired in that moment, but what I told him was the opposite.

"Look, you're a like a brother to me, and I'm not going to fire you. I just can't bring myself to do it," I said. "But if we weren't friends, I would fire you right now."

It was a piercing thing for me to say, but it was how I genuinely felt in that moment. I felt that he needed to hear it from me.

"How do you want to be remembered?" I asked him. "Do you want to be remembered as the guy who has this job because he's the CEO's friend or the guy who has this job because he's the most qualified for it?"

It was the last time we ever had this conversation. Like a true winner, John responded exactly as I had hoped. Even though the words were difficult for me to say, he took them to heart. He spent the next several months putting in extra hours, studying his department and committing himself to becoming the best Vice President of Operations he could be.

Since then, John and I have had our fair share of tough conversations and walks to talk out our differences, but we've never had a "SoHo stroll" that was as dramatic or as severe as that one.

John has turned into a world-class operator and is just as responsible as anyone for our growth and success over the years. He has been promoted many times over, earns considerably more money, and takes on a much more critical role than the one he was hired for five years ago. He is now a high-ranking member of our C-suite executive team.

Through my "SoHo strolls," I've learned to be as direct and brutally honest as I need to be to communicate the message to my subordinates. Sometimes this requires saying things that are piercing, but when you work with great people, they tend to rise to the occasion.

I'm really proud of how far John has come since the day we took that "SoHo stroll." I'm most proud of the fact that he has earned his role today based on his merits, not because he's my friend.

LESSON #77: THE MOST FLATTERING COSTS OF DOING BUSINESS

I learned a valuable lesson in the fall of 2016 about building a successful business: Competitors are going to steal your people, your ideas and your processes.

I used to get annoyed by this, so much that it would often ruin my entire week whenever a competitor would steal our talent or introduce a similar idea to one we had previously launched.

In time, I've changed my perspective on this topic. It no longer annoys me or ruins my week. As I've matured in my career, I've come to realize that this is a sign of flattery. In fact, I view these actions as the most flattering costs of doing business.

All of this came to a head in the fall of 2016, when the strangest confluence of events landed on my desk. On Monday of that week, my financial advisor called me as he was leaving from a meeting with a new client in White Plains, New York.

"Matt, you're not going to believe this," he said. "I just visited with a client and right next door to them was a marketing firm that had almost the same logo as you."

Our logo was such an important and unique part of our company's heritage, so I asked him to take a picture. He proceeded to send me a text message with a picture of the logo, and it turned out he was spot-on. The company he had referenced, a recently launched marketing services start-up, had a logo eerily similar to the one we had been known for since we started our business. This company had made some slight tweaks to the color scheme, but it was clear that they had taken inspiration from our logo, with three circular rings in the center and the initials of the company spread across the circles in a font identical to ours.

It was a bit frustrating for me, as I viewed our logo as an asset that was unique to our company and to our industry. I didn't want to lose our originality.

Later that same week, one of our up-and-coming junior staffers came into my office with a resignation letter in hand. I was shocked he was resigning. He was on the fast-track to getting promoted, making more money and growing into a leadership role. Just a few weeks earlier, we had met for lunch and he seemed thrilled to be working at our company. The employee was emotional as he handed me his resignation letter, and explained that a larger competitor had reached out with an offer he couldn't refuse.

Just when I thought the pain was over, I got hit with another punch to the gut on Friday of that week. Earlier in the year, we had launched a "Year of the Customer" program. Each month, the program showcased an innovative customer service practice from a different blue-chip brand that we implemented for our own customers. It was highly publicized and was recognized as a forward-thinking example of applying innovative customer service practices to a marketing services business. One of my friends got wind of another competitor who had launched something similar and sent me a link to its website. It was obvious that this company had taken our program and modeled its own after ours.

Talk about five days of pain. Across a single week, our competitors had ripped off our logo, poached our people and rolled out a service practice almost identical to the one we had created.

In my younger days, I would've been hot and bothered by this string of events. However, in time I've learned not only to accept it, but to embrace it. Even though it can be annoying when others take your people and your ideas, it's actually the highest form of flattery. It means that you're doing something *right*, and that you're doing something others want to be a part of.

It's simply a flattering cost of doing business.

So, I started to change my perspective on copycats. No longer did I get annoyed by them. Instead, I began to view them as signs that we had built a great company. After all, no competitors would want to take our people or ideas if we had built a losing company.

Thanks to that one crazy week back in 2016, I learned that copycat events are the most flattering costs of doing business.

LESSON #78: KEEP MEMENTOS BY YOUR SIDE

I have found that physical mementos have served an important purpose in my career since the first day I stepped foot in Sony BMG as an entry-level employee in 2005. It was my first real job out of college, and I was thrust right into corporate America without any real sense of what was about to hit me.

Sony BMG's building at 550 Madison Avenue was larger than life. I knew nobody in my department, the cafeteria was bigger than my entire college campus, and the elevator panel had more numbers to choose from than I knew how to count. I felt like a fish out of water in every sense. The whole experience was quite intimidating to me, and I began to look for ways to handle the anxiety.

During this time, I began to carry a needle and thread with me to work as a reminder of my grandfather, who had died the previous year. He was a tailor in the Garment District of Manhattan, and the needle and thread were a physical reminder I could leave on my desk to help me keep things in perspective whenever I felt overwhelmed by the atmosphere of a corporate giant like Sony BMG.

Everywhere I've worked since, I've kept that needle and thread with me. It's been on my desk at every stop of my career, from Sony BMG to my first management role to the day I started our company. It's been with me through four office moves and nearly 4,000 days of running my own business. It's been there on my desk during more than 30,000 client calls, 500 staff meetings, 100 employee onboarding sessions and 40 quarterly earnings reports.

The needle and thread have given me peace and tranquility whenever I've felt anxious and overwhelmed in my career. They've helped me keep things in perspective and served as a reminder of the people who put me in a position to be successful in my career.

Whether it's been the needle and thread or other things, I've found that physical mementos have served an important purpose and have helped me in my career when I've desperately needed a boost.

I've kept every thank you note anyone has ever given me since I started our business. By now, I've accumulated over 1,000 thank you notes from past and present employees, clients, industry peers and people who have reached out to me unsolicited after reading something about our firm. All of these thank you notes hang on a wall in my office, right above the needle and thread. The thank you notes have served as a reminder of the importance of impact in my career. They are constantly in front of me, to remind me that my career is about more than just making money, it's about having an impact on others.

For years, I kept the first check that I ever received from a paying client on the wall in my office. Finally, the accounts payable department called and told me it would void the check if I didn't cash it, but it had a good run of a few years there on my wall. It served as a reminder of how difficult it was to run a business, and as a reminder of the sense of accomplishment you receive as an entrepreneur when a customer chooses to do business with you.

To this day, I have a "bet against" wall in my office, which is a collection of emails, handwritten letters and transcribed voicemails I've received over the years from people who have bet against me or our company. The "bet against" wall is a daily reminder that there will always be doubters, and it serves as motivation to prove the doubters wrong.

Stored away in my desk is a nasty break-up email I received from a girlfriend when I was 22 years old and living at home. The email went something like this:

"I don't date short, skinny guys with receding hairlines who live at home with their parents and have no career prospects."

I saved that email from the moment I received it, knowing that one day I would make her eat her words.

Whether it's a needle and thread, a wall of thank you notes or something else, I've found that physical mementos can serve a real purpose and meaning in your career. Everyone has their own version of the "needle and thread." Keep them by your side.

LESSON #79: EVERYONE COMPLAINS (BUT WINNERS DO IT WITH SOLUTIONS!)

Over the past decade, I've managed all kinds of people, with all different kinds of personalities and all different styles.

Despite what you may have been led to believe, there is one undeniable truth that cuts across all ages, demographics and styles in the workplace:

Everyone complains!

It's human nature, and there's nothing wrong with it.

Here are some of the highlights of the more, shall we say, unique complaints that I've gotten over the years:

"I was at the local police precinct overnight and couldn't make it in on time."

"I can't report to this manager because he has bad B.O."

"If this client calls me a 'snot-nosed kid' again I'm going to lose my mind!"

"The Russian hacker who convinced me to wire $2,000 was really convincing."

"I'm uncomfortable with the floral artwork on the front of the office because it resembles a certain part of the anatomy."

Yes, all of these happened at some point over the past decade.

What is the lesson I have learned? Rather than encouraging subordinates not to complain — something that is unrealistic and that contradicts human nature — I *encourage* them to do the opposite.

That's right. Complain all you want!

There's just one rule:

All complaints *must* have solutions attached to them.

Herein lies the difference between winners and losers in the workplace. I've noticed that losers complain for the sake of complaining, simply to air their grievances and treat the workplace as their personal stage for a bitch fest. They complain without any real actionable steps or suggestions attached to their gripes.

Meanwhile, winners complain with *solutions* attached to them.

Nowadays, I use this as a test to see if someone can cut it on my team. Sometimes I'll throw them a problem that I know they're going to complain about, just to see if they'll simply bitch about it or if they'll come to me with a solution attached. Classic examples of this include capacity levels, tricky client situations or tumultuous relationships with co-workers.

Perhaps you feel overworked because you don't have the resources you need to do your job? Maybe you feel underpaid because that customer isn't compensating you adequately? Perhaps you feel down on your luck because you don't have the chemistry with your co-worker you'd envisioned?

You see, everyone is probably feeling the same way you are in some aspect of their job.

The good news is that we're not talking about detonating an atom bomb. All these issues — and pretty much any other challenge that you're faced with in the workplace — can be fixed pretty quickly and painlessly with some resourcefulness and a solutions-oriented mindset.

The person who feels overworked can probably shuffle some things around or reassess how he's prioritizing things to improve time optimization. Or perhaps he can approach his boss with some proactive ways he can improve his bandwidth levels.

The customer who is underpaying you can probably fork over more money if you provided him with a budget reset. Or perhaps you can approach him with an argument for a budget increase if you support it by objective data that demonstrates the cost-value impact of his relationship with you.

The co-worker you're not getting along with can probably benefit from a one-on-one discussion offsite, so the two of you can find common ground. Or perhaps you could make a few suggestions about how you can adjust your own communication style to complement that of your colleague.

Of course, sometimes the solutions might fall flat on their face, but that's all right, too. Not *every* solution is going to work.

The key, however, is to find people who are willing to look for solutions, not ones who come to you with a gripe every time they're thrown a curve ball.

Remember, *everyone* complains. But the winners complain *with* solutions.

LESSON #80: THE MEANING OF MONEY

If one thing has changed the most dramatically over my first decade in business, it's my viewpoint on money.

As I mentioned in some of the earlier lessons, the younger version of myself was overly concerned with making money when I first started our business. As I've learned in time, my big takeaway is that money is a by-product of hard work and passion, but it should not be the driving factor that motivates you in your career.

I remember legendary investor Ray Dalio talking about his perspective on money. He spoke about money as something you get when you play the "game" of business really well. The point being that your mind should be focused on playing the "game" first and foremost, and that if you do it well, the money will follow. Meanwhile, if your mind is focused first and foremost on making money, then it will be impossible to build anything of consequence. I'm paraphrasing, but this is the gist of what Dalio was saying.

In my opinion, this is a mature and responsible view of money. It is an ideology that took me nearly a decade to adopt, and I wish I'd done it earlier in my career.

Dalio is not the only titan of industry with this point of view. Others include Indra Nooyi, the first female CEO of PepsiCo and the epitome of the American Dream, as well as Jamie Dimon, Bob Iger, Oprah Winfrey and many others.

As I've advanced in my career, I've noticed that the most successful people I've been exposed to share one thing in common: They view money as an output, not an input. Their primary focus is on being great at their craft, whether that's running a company, being a successful, on-air talent, or rising through the ranks of management. They all share a passion, purpose and hunger when it comes to their jobs. They are driven by this passion, not by the money.

Of course, it's easy to roll your eyes and say that it's convenient for billionaires and highly successful Fortune 500 CEOs to espouse how meaningless money is to them. However, the deeper you look, the more apparent it becomes that their philosophy is valid.

In my career, my passion has become my main driver. To paraphrase Dalio, I have come to absolutely love playing the "game" as my career has evolved. In my case, the "game" is building and running our business. I am more passionate about it and derive a greater sense of purpose and meaning from it now than ever before.

The most interesting observation I've had about money is that my greatest financial gain has come during those times I have played the game the best, where my focus was on the work, not on making money. The money has been a welcome by-product of doing a really good job of playing the game.

Once I switched my mindset and started prioritizing playing the game over making money, my career and business skyrocketed. I have felt a deeper sense of purpose, have had an insatiable thirst for improvement, and have been squarely focused on becoming the best version of myself that I can possibly be in the workplace, not the richest version of myself. It just so happens that once I adopted that mindset, I also started to make the most money.

Of all the things I've done to evolve and pivot over the past 10 years, my viewpoint on money is the pivot that has brought me the most gratification and sense of meaning.

I'm so happy to have fallen in love with playing the "game." The better I do it, the more confident I am that the money will keep following. But never again will I put money first.

LESSON #81: THE IMPORTANCE OF SCENARIOS AND PRESSURE TESTING

Back in 2017, we conceived the vision for a rewards model that would enable our employees to choose their own rewards based on what motivated them the most. Today, Pace Points, as it's known, is one of our greatest examples of innovation in action.

Here's how Pace Points works. Our employees accumulate points for individual, team and company achievements. They are then able to cash in their points for rewards across any of six categories that motivate them the most. The categories are cash, travel, experiences, health and wellness, transportation, and quality of life. Rewards range from a few hundred dollars all the way up to $50,000 in each category.

Now in its third year, Pace Points has been a source of great pride for our company and for our employees. Each year, the program gets bigger and better and we make improvements. CNN, CBS and *Forbes* have showcased Pace Points as one of the most innovative and forward-thinking examples of employee rewards and culture programs today.

Our employees have redeemed points for incredible trips and experiences, including weeklong vacations to Asia and the Caribbean, annual commuting-expense vouchers, monthly grocery passes and tech products like laptops, state-of-the-art speaker systems and mobile devices.

The reason I bring up the program is to illustrate a point. Behind our greatest example of innovation was a rigorous, thorough and elaborate process that included comprehensive scenario and pressure testing.

By the time Pace Points was ready for showtime in 2018, we had already spent a year of testing it rigorously. The process might not have been very sexy, but it was absolutely necessary. It proved to us the importance of running pressure tests and scenarios before we rolled out an initiative of this magnitude.

Before we rolled out the program, we dedicated an entire year to running pressure tests and scenarios.

During this period, our Chief Financial Officer handled each of the financial aspects of the behind-the-scenes work. This included a yearlong dress rehearsal where he applied Pace Points to every employee as if the program were already up and running. He also studied each of the financial nuances of the program, including best practices for how to handle the accounting methodology, expense accruals, forfeitures impact, and assigning values to each of the cash and non-cash rewards.

Additionally, he ran scenarios based on the potential redemption behaviors of our employees so we could be prepared for any and all situations that might arise when it came time for our employees to redeem their points.

Our head of operations handled each of the logistical aspects of the testing phase. This included administrative planning, potential technological glitches, patent and trademark submission processes, and how to book travel arrangements for the bigger-ticket rewards.

I worked hand-in-hand with the heads of all our departments to appropriately calibrate and model the points structure and commensurate reward options. I also worked with them to solicit feedback from our employees on the rewards they most wanted to see included in the program.

Thank the Lord we spent the entire year to run pressure tests and conduct scenario planning. If it had not been for this exercise, the entire program would have been a disaster and likely would've crippled our company from a financial standpoint.

During the testing phase, we discovered more holes in the program than we could've ever imagined. Details that we hadn't prepared for emerged, including how we would manage short-term versus long-term trip planning, how we would handle employees who terminated with Pace Points left in their banks, and the frequency and cadence of redemption opportunities.

These all turned out to be small but critically important details. If we had launched the program before troubleshooting these issues, it would have fallen flat on its face, we wouldn't have been adequately prepared to handle the logistical demands, and the company would've been financially liable to the point of no return.

Today, Pace Points is a source of great pride. It is something that I will take with me for the rest of my career, knowing that we went toe-to-toe with rewards and innovation programs from the largest companies in the world and we beat them with our innovation. I am very proud that we created it, and that it stands as a beacon of our willingness to experiment and invent. It is also a great example of teamwork, seeing so many different departments come together to bring it to life.

And it would never have been possible without rigorous scenarios and pressure testing.

Next time you have a big idea, make sure you're spending just as much time on *testing* it out as you are on rolling it out.

LESSON #82: COMPETE AND CARE

When it comes to recruiting, I've learned there is no such thing as *perfect* talent. There is, however, talent that is perfect for your *culture*. Herein lies the key to building a great team in the workplace.

Don't worry about finding the perfect talent. Worry about finding the talent that is perfect for *you*.

Every company has its own identity and its own culture that is unique to them. I've learned that as you scale, you need to recruit people who embody the identity and culture that are unique to you. Sometimes this means having to turn down perfectly talented and qualified professionals simply because they didn't fit your unique cultural identity.

What's the unique cultural identity of our company you ask?

Compete and Care, est. 2010.

As we began the journey to scale our business in 2010, I learned that in order for us to win, we were going to have to recruit talent that was both competitive and caring. It seems like such an easy balance to find, but in reality, we've found that only a select few embody *Compete and Care* virtues.

Here's how we arrived at our unique cultural identity.

When we started searching for talent in 2010, I quickly learned that the marketing agency employment scene in New York is about as cutthroat as it gets. Back then, as is still the case today, the agency environment was fast, demanding and intense. You couldn't succeed in the city's agency environment unless you had competitive genes in your DNA. You would get swallowed alive if you weren't a fierce competitor.

We found that candidates we interviewed from other agencies were uber competitive, Type A personalities and they wanted to win for themselves.

In a vacuum, these were good traits, but not when it came at the expense of the *team*.

Many of the candidates we interviewed clearly had the "compete" part of the equation, but were lacking the "care" part of it. We overlooked the "compete" part when we first started hiring. Consequently, we made some bad hires and quickly learned that competitiveness and individuality were toxic and counterproductive for our culture when they were not offset by an equal dose of *caring*.

On the other end of the spectrum were the candidates who were caring but not competitive. We found some candidates who clearly had the right temperament, disposition and energy to be successful on our team. They had been burned by previous agency experiences and were looking to find a place they could call home for a long time to come. They were perfectly well-mannered, but they lacked the competitive gene required to win in this environment.

So, we ended up making a few bad hires by offering candidates who embodied the "care" part of the equation but were lacking the "compete" part of it. We learned that they had an equally negative effect on our culture as the overly competitive candidates. The "care" candidates ended up being great-attitude people, but lacked the competitive drive and killer instinct required to win.

This is how our *Compete and Care* slogan was born.

In our early dealings with candidates, we learned that if we were going to win, we were going to have to recruit talent that had a strong balance of competitiveness as well as the ability to care for their teammates. We started running checks and balances in the recruiting process to test the candidates on their *Compete and Care* abilities. For every question we asked to test their competitiveness, we offset it with a role-playing scenario to test out if this was an individual who possessed the care and selflessness required to be a successful member of our team.

In the early years, I gave everyone a *Compete and Care* score following their interview. If they didn't meet the minimum score requirements, we didn't hire them, no matter how talented they were. We ended up passing on some very talented individuals who didn't pass muster on the "care" part, and we also passed on some incredibly team-oriented candidates who didn't cut it on the "compete" part. Even though it was tough to pass up on some of this talent at the time, we were building a unique cultural identity that would set the foundation for years to come.

A decade later, and *Compete and Care* still remains our unique cultural identity. *Compete and Care* continues to serve as our core philosophy that guides all of our recruiting decisions. We even have a fancy *Compete and Care* lounge, complete with individual and team-oriented trophies and mementos that embody the essence of what it means to *Compete and Care.*

The lesson here is to be true to your unique cultural identity, and recruit with that identity in mind. Don't ever compromise your unique cultural identity when bringing talent onto your team.

LESSON #83: EMBRACE THE PACE

As the title of this book would suggest, I'm a bit partial to this lesson.

I have always worked fast. *Very* fast. My preference has always been to work at a high-octane speed. Some might even say that I operate at breakneck speed, but I wouldn't have it any other way. I've always felt the workday was more exhilarating when I attacked it in an all-out-blitz sort of way, just like the '85 Bears.

Little did I know that my penchant for speed would later turn into one of our company's greatest competitive differentiators and our best-known unique selling proposition (USP).

Back when I was first starting out in business, I learned that my fast-paced approach served me well. I was able to multitask and wear the many hats required of a start-up entrepreneur. I was able to juggle everything — including sales, service, back-office operations, recruiting, logistical and administrative tasks — and do it all in a fast and overall efficient manner.

Additionally, I was able to service clients in a much faster and more expedient way than my larger competitors. While they were busy filling out time sheets and keeping track of their hours, I was moving fast to show value and drive results for my clients.

Before I knew it, word of my speed was spreading among prospects in my network. Everywhere I went, people would look at me and say, "Hey, you're the kid who moves really fast, right?" Suddenly, everyone started to view me as a scrappy, fast-paced operator.

It seems crazy now, but back then speed was not viewed as an advantage in our industry.

Historically, marketing service agencies operated on the "billable hour" model, where speed was viewed as a disadvantage to the service provider. The more hours the agency racked up on behalf of a client, the more money it got paid. It was a model that completely disincentivized the agency from working fast. In fact, it was built in direct contrast to the interests of the client, rewarding the agency for working slower and logging more hours on a given account.

I found that I was onto something with this speed-first model. Clients liked it, prospects were attracted to it, and our staff seemed to enjoy working in a fast-paced environment where they were absolved of any responsibility to fill out time sheets or keep track of their hours.

Speed was clearly turning into a competitive differentiator, and my strongest USP.

Back then, there were really no marketing service agencies touting speed as a differentiator. I saw an opportunity and exploited it to the fullest. From that point forward, we made speed central to our strategy, positioning and differentiation in a highly competitive marketplace.

That's the genesis of "Embrace the Pace," which remains our slogan to this day, one that has been well-received by staff, clients and prospects alike. We trademarked our slogan in 2016, and since then have fielded dozens of inquiries from other companies, sports franchises and trade groups wanting to purchase the name.

We touted our speed-first model over the standard, "billable hour" model in our new business pitches. Our t-shirts and swag all pointed back to speed. Our website and marketing collateral all used images that were associated with speed. We turned our conference room into the "Pace Room." Our office was decorated with pictures of Ferraris, Lockheed SR-71 Blackbirds and champion thoroughbreds. Our customer service policies all traced back to rapid-response and real-time feedback.

Everything we did was fast. Everything we did was based on speed. There was nobody who was going to work faster than us. We literally "Embraced the Pace" in every sense.

But "Embrace the Pace" is no longer just a slogan. It has become a mindset. It stands for a lifestyle in the workplace that proves how exhilarating and rewarding your career can be if you embrace it head-on with positive energy.

The big lesson I learned here is that when you see an opportunity to differentiate yourself from your competitors, you should go for it. Sometimes your greatest USP will come from something that seems so natural to you, yet is such a foreign concept to your competitors. For me, it was my speed. For you, it might be something else. Perhaps it's your customer friendliness, your sophistication or your pricing.

Whatever it is, make sure you capitalize on it and use it as the centerpiece of your competitive differentiation in the marketplace.

"Embrace the Pace," baby. That's my USP. It's fast, it's exhilarating, and most importantly, it's different.

LESSON #84: START AND END STRONG

By March 2010, things were busy. I had signed five clients and was getting ready to move my operation from my basement into a new, shared workspace in midtown Manhattan. I needed to start looking for people to hire. On top of all this, my wife and I were expecting our first daughter, Viviana.

Life was great and things were exciting, but it was busy, to say the least. I needed to figure out a way to manage the workload in addition to helping my wife, who was ready to go into labor literally any minute.

With all the chaos that came with managing a one-person start-up, I needed to make sure I didn't drop the ball on my bread-and-butter business, which was my client account work. All the other components of starting a business — sales, recruiting, back-office administration, operations —were new to me. These were the components of the business that I needed to spend time on in order to grow to the next level. However, the fact remained that if I were going to stay in business, I couldn't let the ball drop on servicing the clients that were paying my bills. I couldn't allow any of the non-service-related components of entrepreneurship come at the expense of jeopardizing my paying clients.

During this time, I developed *Start and End Strong,* which has been a guiding customer service principle of our company.

I managed my time so that each day, first thing in the morning, I was forced to deliver good news to every client I was servicing. Then I forced myself to deliver good news to every client at the end of the day as well. The thought being that, if the first thing a client thinks of his service experience in the morning is positive and the last thing he thinks of it before he shuts down for the day is also positive, how upset could he possibly be with his service experience?

Start and End Strong worked, and it worked big. It enabled me to manage my time so that all of my clients were taken care of and happy while I was still able to focus on the other parts of growing my business during the day. It was a subconscious tactic, but it worked effectively.

Without exception, every client received good news from me to start the day and to end the day. The good news could, for example, be an account result, a strategic idea, a consultative recommendation, a piece of competitive intelligence, or a valuable report or data initiative.

Start and End Strong gave me discipline in my client service approach and provided a blueprint for keeping client satisfaction at a high level while I was managing other parts of our business.

Think about all of your dealings with vendors, service providers and retailers. Take one of your favorite stores, for example. If the first thing you thought of when you walked into that store was positive and the last thing you thought of when you walked out was positive, chances are you would come back to that store again, right? This is the same concept behind *Start and End Strong*. I've found it to be an effective approach that has transferred successfully over to client service businesses such as my own.

Even though it started in my basement when I was a sole proprietor, *Start and End Strong* has stayed with us through the years. It has become one of our main customer service principles and it has differentiated our service experience from those of our competitors and other vendors. Our entire account management operation is trained to put *Start and End Strong* into practice for our clients each day, and to make sure that the first and last thing the client hears from us is positive news.

If you're in a customer-facing role, commit to starting and ending each day with good news for your customers. I'm willing to bet that your customer satisfaction levels will increase, your time management skills will improve, and you'll differentiate your service approach from those of your competitors and industry peers.

Start and End Strong. All day, every day.

LESSON #85: I WAS WRONG

On December 3, 2009, I sat down for breakfast at the Grand Hyatt Hotel near Grand Central with a well-known executive in the media services industry. I had a great deal of respect and admiration for him. He was somebody who had achieved tremendous success in my industry, and was viewed by many as a legendary figure. I was shocked that I was even in the same room as him.

A few weeks earlier, I had taken a "Foul Shot" to him, which ultimately led to the breakfast (see "Lesson #3: Take Foul Shots"). I had introduced myself, explaining that I was a young, aspiring entrepreneur looking to build an agency and would love to meet with him to get his advice and perspectives. I didn't expect anything to come from the outreach, but sure enough, a few weeks later, his assistant got in touch, informing me that the executive would be in New York in a few weeks and would be happy to have breakfast.

Talk about an incredible gesture of time and paying it forward on his part. He had no reason to meet with a no-name, unestablished kid like me, but he agreed to do it.

I was so nervous the night before the meeting. I recited my lines in the mirror, rehearsed the questions I would ask him, and flipped through my 30-page business plan all night long with my sweaty palms.

Our meeting was set for 7 o'clock at the hotel. I took the 5 o'clock commuter train from Westchester into Manhattan so I wouldn't run any risk whatsoever of being late. He arrived for the meeting and we shook hands. I was in awe. It was like shaking the hand of a giant. Through the years, I've met so many important people, including celebrities and corporate bigwigs, that I've become numb to these meetings. I am no longer awestruck anytime I meet someone of note. However, as a 26-year-old pipsqueak, this was a huge deal to me. I felt like I was meeting a Hollywood star.

He turned out to be incredibly humble, empathetic and down to earth. He had a soft spot for young entrepreneurs who wanted to start something on their own. He was very generous with his time, insights and advice. I spent the next 45 minutes answering questions that he asked about my vision, business model and growth plan, and then shutting up and listening intently to his responses.

Toward the end of the breakfast, he paused as we waited for the bill.

"Matt, you are going to be a successful entrepreneur," he said. "I have no doubts about that."

I was flattered and honored. It was like receiving a blessing from the Pope and gave me assurance that I was on the right track.

"Thank you so much," I replied. "That means a lot to me."

Then he paused again, put down his napkin, and continued to speak.

"However, I wouldn't start this business if I were you," he said. "You brought me here for my honest advice, and that is my brutally honest advice to you."

Talk about a dagger right to my core. To this day, those words still make me cringe whenever I think about them, just like nails on a chalkboard.

He went on to tell me why he didn't think it was a smart idea to start the business. We were in the midst of a recession, so there were economic barriers he warned me about. I was young and inexperienced, with only a few years of work under my belt, so he advised me to gain more experience and build my Rolodex. I had no financial backing or capital reserves of consequence, so he urged me to build a small war chest of capital so I could withstand a few months of operating losses.

"You're going to be a great entrepreneur," he said. "Just not right now."

The truth is, I couldn't argue with any of his advice. It was reasoned, articulate and clearly coming from someone who knew what it took to be a successful entrepreneur.

However, like all entrepreneurs, you need to go with your gut, and my gut told me to go for it. After all, I was a stubborn Italian kid from New York, and I was going to do this no matter what anybody told me.

The next month I started the business, and the rest is history.

I sent the executive a note after our meeting, thanking him for his time and advice. I told him that I had decided to start the business and that I would keep him posted on my progress.

Years passed and I never heard back from him, and understandably so. He was a busy executive who traveled the world and probably met with thousands of people every year far more important than I was.

Fast-forward to 2013, and we were named one of the 50 fastest-growing firms in the United States. We had a celebration in the office and issued a press release announcing the achievement. When I got home to my family that night, my BlackBerry buzzed (yes, BlackBerry devices were still en vogue back then!). To my amazement, it was a note from the executive I had met with over breakfast all those years earlier. I was shocked he even remembered me. There was no subject line, and just three words in the body of the email. The words were in all caps:

"I WAS WRONG."

He recalled our meeting and the advice he had shared with me. I couldn't believe he remembered that conversation. It was probably the most gratifying note I had ever received. It was validation that I had made the right decision, and that we had beat the odds.

Even though his message was just three words, it was the perfect response. It captured the essence of what the entrepreneurial journey — and your career journey — are all about. Go with your gut, let your instincts guide you, and don't forget that every day is a quest to prove somebody wrong.

Out of all the decisions I've been wrong about in my career, I'm happy to say that I was right about that one.

LESSON #86: CHAMPIONSHIP MONTHS

My second daughter, Valentina, was born on July 8, 2011. It was a typically sweltering New York summer Friday. After spending quality time with my wife and newborn daughter over the weekend at Methodist Hospital in Brooklyn, I was right back to work on Monday.

I'm embarrassed to admit it now, but back then I was relieved that she was born on a Friday so I didn't have to miss valuable workdays. That's how dumb and narrow-minded I was when I was first getting our business started. It's a big regret of mine, and if I had a newborn child at this stage of my life, I would definitely take more time to enjoy him or her — certainly more than just a weekend!

One good thing did come out of my workaholic mindset back in those days, however:

Championship Months.

Our business wasn't even two years old at that point, and I was hungry for more clients. As soon as I got back to the office on Monday, I began cold pitching prospects. Typically, my response rate on cold pitches was very low, in the single digits. However, for some reason, prospects were responding to me at a much higher clip that day. I thought it had something to do with destiny since my daughter had just been born, but it wasn't destiny.

It was *Championship Months.*

I was also in full recruiting mode that week, as we had two positions we needed to fill. We were a start-up business with virtually no reputation, so my response rate on recruiting pitches was, like those of my cold prospect pitches, very low. Rarely if ever did any recruiting prospects respond to one of my cold pitches. To my pleasant surprise, however, more than 15 candidates responded. Again, I was convinced that my newborn daughter had brought me good luck, but it wasn't luck.

It was *Championship Months.*

I was also in upsell mode that week, as we were trying to get our third quarter kickstarted with a revenue windfall. I began reaching out to existing clients, trying to convince them to expand their scopes of work and to spend more money with us ahead of the fourth-quarter rush. My success rate on upsells was pathetic. If I got three clients to agree to an upsell over the first 18 months of our business it was generous. Again, to my surprise, I was able to convert four clients to larger packages at higher price points. As if I needed any more reason to love my beautiful newborn daughter, now she was sending good vibes my way in the form of upsell revenue. But this had nothing to do with good vibes.

This had to do with *Championship Months*.

Cold pitches that never went answered suddenly were being well-received. Employee candidates who usually didn't show me the time of day were returning my calls. Upsell opportunities with existing clients who normally brushed me off were now saying yes to spending more money with us.

Why was this happening?

I started to investigate, made a few calls, and what became clear to me was that I was the *only* service provider who was working that week. While everyone else was out partying at the Hamptons, relaxing on the beach or taking an extended Independence Day vacation, I was busy hustling, working my ass off. And it was paying off.

I wasn't doing anything particularly brilliant or earth shattering. I was doing the same thing that I always did. It's just that I was the *only* one who was doing it during that week and the following weeks. I learned that the summer months were *Championship Months*. The volume of pitches that these folks were used to receiving was exponentially lower during *Championship Months*. Therefore, the odds of them responding to me was exponentially higher during these times.

A few months later, I repeated the same exercise during the week between Christmas and New Year's Day, which was a historically slow work week. To my surprise, my outreach efforts produced the same results as they did over the summer months. Sales prospects were responding to me at a higher clip, employee candidates were returning my calls with greater frequency, and existing clients were listening to my upsell pitches.

These times — the summer months, holiday months and slower months — were clearly my *Championship Months*. These were the months I would outwork my competitors, and the results would pay dividends. They would make my year, and create winning opportunities for me and my company that separated us from the pack.

In your career, championship opportunities will be created during *Championship Months*. Commit to outworking the competition during the *Championship Months* and it is a guaranteed formula for success. (Plus, a little bit of luck from a newborn baby can never hurt.)

LESSON #87: DO THE LITTLE THINGS

In 2015, we signed global telecommunications powerhouse Airtel as a client. Airtel was a multibillion-dollar company based in India with a footprint in nearly every country in the world. However, it was not as well-known in the U.S. market as AT&T, Verizon and other competitors, so it hired our firm to raise its profile domestically. It was a big coup for us, as it gave us legitimacy and showed us that we could go toe-to-toe with global competitors for enterprise accounts and beat them.

However, we would have lost the account had we not done the *littlest* thing.

Before winning the account in 2015, we had been pursuing Airtel for quite a while. We had a few false starts in previous years but had made it all the way to the finish line in 2014, before we lost the account to a global firm with which Airtel had a long relationship. When Airtel invited us to compete for its business again the following year, I was determined to win the account.

After a few initial phone calls and meetings, Airtel's management team had narrowed its list of finalists down to our firm and one larger competitor. I had some connections in the telecommunications industry, including a relationship with a consulting firm called APTelecom. I sat on APTelecom's board, and its CEO Eric Handa had a relationship with Airtel's CEO.

During the same time period Airtel was expected to make its decision, the annual Pacific Telecommunications Council (PTC) tradeshow was taking place in Hawaii. PTC is a "who's who" for the telecommunications industry. Each January, thousands of important telecom executives fly in from across the world to discuss their goals for the year at PTC over luaus, golf outings and beachside cocktail events overlooking the Pacific Ocean. It's not a bad club to be in, if you can get in!

Eric knew we were a finalist for the Airtel business and wanted to help us win. He encouraged me to come out to Hawaii for PTC so he could introduce me to Airtel's CEO and other members of its management team.

Naturally, I made the trip. In addition to the opportunity to close the Airtel business, there was no way that I was going to pass up a trip to Hawaii in January! I booked the first flight out to Honolulu with my wife, figuring we would turn the trip into a part-work, part-pleasure getaway.

The night before I was going to meet with Airtel, its marketing chief asked me to put together a few slides with some recommendations on how our firm would help to enhance its profile in the U.S. We had already delivered a formal proposal and presentation to the company, but its marketing representative now wanted to see crystallized ideas and specific recommendations.

I stayed up late in my hotel room that evening coming up with some creative angles and messages I thought would resonate with consumers in the U.S. One of the ideas involved getting Airtel's mid-level regional managers more exposure to the press and positioning its young talent as more innovative and technologically advanced than those from larger players in the market.

The next morning, as I was preparing for the meeting, I showed Eric the slides.

"Take this one out!" he exclaimed, referring to the slide about promoting its mid-level managers and younger talent in the U.S.

Airtel was an Indian company, and Eric went on to explain that Indian business customs are very traditional and hierarchical. Suggesting we would promote the company's junior talent publicly would likely turn off the Airtel management team and demonstrate that we didn't have an understanding of or respect for business customs in their home country.

Naturally, I removed the slide immediately, and the meeting in Hawaii with Airtel's management team was productive. Our firm made a great impression on them, and we ended up winning the account a few months later. It was a big achievement for us, as it marked the first time we had won an account from a multibillion-dollar brand when we were competing directly against global firms.

This taught me a valuable lesson about the importance of doing the little things. Had Eric not been there to bail me out, I would've missed a critically important detail and we would've surely lost the Airtel account. At an executive level, I should have been diligent enough to catch this detail on my own. One simple Google search would have armed me with all the information I needed to avoid making this mistake.

Sometimes the difference between winning and losing in the workplace comes down to the smallest details. Whether it's taking the extra time to research business customs for a foreign prospect (as was the case with Airtel) or other things such following up meetings with thank you notes, ensuring there are no spelling errors on presentation materials or double-checking names to make sure you pronounce them properly, the little things matter.

Sweat the details. Doing the *little things* will lead to *big* outcomes.

LESSON #88: FOOD IS NOURISHING, MEALS ARE GALVANIZING

Growing up Italian-American in New York, it's impossible for your life *not* to revolve around food.

Turkey was merely window dressing on Thanksgiving. The *real* Thanksgiving meal was a continuous flow of antipasto, lasagna and cheesecake until eventually you exploded. Christmas Day was just a continuation of the prior night's feast of fish, and the words "I'm full" were actually translated as "you need another plate" in the dialect of old-school New York Italians. Meals were never over until zippers popped, and a fresh jar of *Brioschi* (the Italian version of Alka-Seltzer) was always served to wash down the contents of the meal.

Even if I gained 10 pounds over the summer, my grandmother would tell me I was "losing weight." And God forbid I *didn't* put on a few pounds before the school year started — that was immediate grounds for a psychological evaluation and a head examination.

This was my life growing up. My greatest childhood memories are over food, typically in a family setting, all of us sitting at one table.

When I started our business in 2010, I wanted to establish many of these family-style traditions at the company. I saw firsthand the galvanizing impact food could have on family and other loved ones, so I figured it could serve the same purpose in the workplace.

Even though budgets were tight in the early days, we found a way to scrape together enough money to pay for everyone's lunch on Thursday. The staff got to choose from any local restaurant. There was only one rule: We had to eat *together*.

I learned quickly that, just like with family, food brought our team closer together in the workplace. Correction: It wasn't *food* that brought us together — it was *meals* that brought us together.

I learned that food is *nourishing*, but meals are *galvanizing*.

Food itself doesn't do anything to bring people closer. It's sharing meals, interacting and exchanging stories that inspire unity among people. Our lunch tradition was a great way to create bonds and team chemistry in the early days. We were just a few people nestled into a shared office in midtown Manhattan, but through our weekly meal together, we were able to learn about one another, discuss goals for the company and develop the chemistry that is so essential during the start-up phase.

Our weekly lunch is still happening, and it continues to be a source of excitement among our employees. Everybody wants to see what's on the menu each week and looks forward to interacting with their teammates over food. In fact, I can't recall any week we ever skipped our Thursday lunch.

Beyond our Thursday lunch, we've grown our meals budget considerably over the years. Now we also have pizza Fridays, monthly custom omelet stations, Thanksgiving team meals and my personal favorite, our Seis de Mayo celebration, our own version of Cinco de Mayo, complete with a mariachi band, margaritas and Mexican specialties.

In our earlier days, when our team was much smaller, my mother-in-law Teresa used to come into the office a few times a year and cook for the staff. The meals were extravagant and everybody loved them. They usually consisted of homemade wine and sausage, fresh pasta, eggplant parmesan and pastries from the legendary Villabate Alba on 18th Avenue in Brooklyn. The staff got a real kick out of it, and some of our most galvanizing moments came during these meals.

Even in one-on-one settings, I've always preferred to conduct my most important meetings over meals. Quarterly budget meetings, monthly executive offsites with my Chief Operating Officer, annual performance reviews with my direct reports, management retreats and goal-setting sessions — each of these is conducted over a meal. I've found it brings my direct reports and me closer together and creates a relatability and a connection between us that is difficult to replicate in an office environment.

I'm sure if you look back on your career, you'll find that some of your most memorable moments with co-workers have happened over meals. Not over *food*, but over *meals*.

Food is nourishing, but meals are *galvanizing*. That's a lesson I've learned since childhood and that has served me well in the workplace.

LESSON #89: THE CLIENT VALUE MATRIX

In 2012, I learned an important lesson about how to determine the true value of your customers.

We were approached by a start-up technology company looking for a public relations firm. The prospect had just completed a friends and family round of funding and could only afford to pay our company $2,500 per month, which was well below our minimum rates.

The prospect was referred to us by one of our venture capital connections who was considering making an investment in the start-up once it advanced to the next round of funding. Its technology was innovative, its leadership team was smart and it seemed like it had a great business model.

The prospect offered me a small piece of equity in the company to offset the lower retainer fees, with assurances that the company would increase the retainer once it closed its next round of funding. Cash flow was king back in those days (it still is today!), so naturally I declined the account in favor of signing a higher-paying prospect in our pipeline.

Talk about a *huge* mistake.

Three months later, the prospect raised a $5 million Series A round. Six months after that, it raised a $20 million Series B round. Along the way, it built out its solution and turned it into one of the earliest examples of artificial intelligence for enterprise brands.

The next year, IBM acquired the company and integrated it into what is today known as the IBM Watson suite of solutions, one of the premier providers of AI and machine learning technology. That small slice of equity would likely have been worth millions, we would have been in pole position to establish a relationship with IBM, and in the blink of an eye, the $2,500 retainer would have grown considerably higher.

Instead, I declined the account for a higher paying client that ended up going bankrupt after six months and left us with a collections nightmare.

I lacked the vision to see beyond the small retainer fee, and it turned out to be a wasted opportunity. It also taught me an important lesson about the need to look at more than just fees when you assess the true value of a customer. Sure, cash is an important consideration, but it isn't the only consideration.

After this experience, I was committed to developing a system so we wouldn't make the same mistake again.

With this in mind, I created a client value matrix. I took a series of six variables that would determine the value of a client. Cash fees was one of the variables. The others included timely payment, access to new networking contacts, referral opportunities, growth potential and my personal favorite, the PIA factor (PIA stands for "pain in the ass"). I then assigned scores to each of the categories. In aggregate, whichever clients and prospects had the highest scores would be the most valuable clients.

The client value matrix became an important tool that helped our management team assess which prospects to sign, and which active clients would get the most TLC from us. It wasn't a perfect system, but it was much better than the non-existent system we had in place beforehand.

We've leaned on the client value matrix frequently since we first developed it. Some of our most successful client exits to companies such as Dentsu, Gartner, Google and Workday all came as a result of prospects that we assessed through the client value matrix. Similarly, some of our wisest decisions to reduce, modify or terminate active clients came as a result of the scores from the client value matrix.

The client value matrix should be customized according to each business. The variables that make a client valuable to one business might not be the same as the ones that make a client valuable to another business. For example, a business that operates on thin margins and one that is dependent on cash flow will likely prioritize payment terms and cash fees over everything else in its client value matrix. On the other hand, a business that is backed by venture capital and that can withstand dips in cash flow will likely prioritize growth potential and access to new networking contacts in its client value matrix.

I'm sure glad we created the client value matrix back in 2012. I just wish it hadn't had to come at such a steep price.

LESSON #90: THE RELATIONSHIP OF CHILDREN AND CAREERS

One of the most powerful lessons I've learned over the past decade was taught to me by my daughter Viviana when she was just eight years old.

My three daughters, Viviana, Valentina and Simona, were born in March 2010, July 2011 and June 2013, respectively. All three of them have essentially grown up with my business. They know me as dad around the house, but professionally they know me only as the founder of my business. For their entire lives I've been the founder and CEO of N6A, and that's the only professional title with which they associate me. They have been surrounded by my business every day in some way, shape or form since they were born.

However, perhaps none of my daughters is as inextricably linked to my business as my eldest daughter, Viviana, who was born just a few short months after I started the company.

On March 25, 2010, I was in the delivery room at Methodist Hospital in Brooklyn as my wife gave birth to Viviana. I was brand new to entrepreneurship and I was brand new to fatherhood. I look at my daughter now and she is a beautiful, confident young girl who is entering her pre-teen years. As our business has grown, so has she. Just like I've learned valuable lessons about entrepreneurship over the past decade, I've learned infinitely more lessons about fatherhood. Those are the lessons that are most important to me, not the ones I've learned about being a better professional. Ironically, through my professional work, she taught me an important lesson about fatherhood.

As everyone who has started a new job, career or business at the same time they're having a child can attest, the relationship between children and careers are inextricably linked. When children and careers grow up on parallel tracks, you often remember life events and associate them with career milestones. People have a way of remembering specific life events and associating them with new jobs, new career beginnings and new professional milestones.

For example, the morning before my oldest daughter was born, I remember hiring our first employee. The day after her baptism, I remember we signed our first office lease, and on her first birthday we won a major industry award. I remember her taking her first steps not in my living room but in my office. I remember her picking up the phones for our employees once she learned to talk, taking the train into the office with me every summer, and sitting in a cardboard box when we moved into our first office.

I used to be ashamed and disappointed that I couldn't remember my daughter's life events without associating them with my business. I used to feel like Viviana got the short end of the stick because her father was always thinking about work in some capacity, and it was difficult for me to separate my business entirely whenever we shared a life event.

I used to feel guilty — that is before Viviana taught me an important lesson in 2018.

At the time, I was debating whether to sell our company to an interested party. I decided to share the news with Viviana.

"Daddy might sell the company," I told her.

Of course, my daughter didn't understand the economics or any of the *professional* consequences that would come along with the decision to sell the firm, but she immediately understood the *life* consequences. She went on to tell me how content she was with her life, and she remembered so many of the same life moments that she and I had shared in my workplace.

In that moment, it was clear to me how much she associated my business with her childhood. The most gratifying part as a father was that, all her memories were positive and demonstrated that she had learned important life lessons through her exposure to my work. She looked at my business, and in her own 8-year-old mind, it was clear that she associated it with life lessons that build the character and values that all parents want their children to have. Values like female empowerment and equality in the workforce, financial risk taking, and the power of self-belief and self-confidence.

These were values that were important not just on a professional level but also on a personal level.

In that moment, it was clear to me that through my work, I had impacted my daughter in a meaningful way. From that point forward, I stopped feeling so guilty about taking my work home with me.

My daughter taught me a valuable lesson about the relationship of children and careers. She taught me that your career can be one of the most powerful platforms for teaching your kids the most important lessons a parent can teach.

Thank you, Viviana, for teaching me this lesson. I love you.

LESSON #91: DON'T BE AFRAID TO ASK

Sometimes, the toughest thing you can do in your career is to ask a question. I know that sounds crazy, but some of the most regrettable outcomes in my career could have been avoided if I had just asked a simple question.

Here's the lesson I've learned.

Don't be afraid to ask!

If it's on your mind, you should ask it. It always works out better this way.

Are you a salesperson? If so, ask the prospect what it will take to earn his or her business. Ask if they'll give you more money if you stand by your product. Ask who else you're competing against.

Are you a client services representative? If so, ask the customer if he or she is happy. Ask what you can be doing a better job of. Ask how you can improve.

Perhaps you're an entry-level employee who's looking to take the next step in your career? If this is the case, ask your manager what it will take to get to the next level. Ask how you can make more money. Ask how you can take on more responsibility.

Maybe you're a senior executive who reports directly into the CEO? If this is the case, ask the CEO that question that's been on your mind. Ask how you can improve your reporting relationship.

Maybe you're an IT person who's looking to switch over to operations? If so, ask the department head how you can make the switch. Ask what you need to study. Ask which skills you should acquire in order to be successful in the new role.

In my experience, when you *ask*, you usually *receive*. You don't ever want to leave anything to chance. Closure and definitiveness are important, and if you don't ask, you'll never know what it takes to receive the big outcome that you've been looking for.

If you're the salesperson, how can you possibly close that big prospect unless you know what it's going to take to earn that business? If you're the client services representative, how can you improve for the customer if you're not asking what it's going to take? If you're the entry-level employee, how can you take the next step unless you ask your manager how to do so?

So many of the mistakes that I've made through the years have come when I've been afraid to ask the question. Sometimes I've been too shy to ask. Sometimes I've been afraid of what the response would be. Sometimes I've simply been too lazy to ask. As I look back on those mistakes — lost clients, lost employees, lost sales prospects — so many of the outcomes would have been completely different if I had just asked the simple question that was on my mind.

In 2016, we were pitching America's Test Kitchen, one of the largest media companies in the world specializing in cooking and culinary arts. It was a big opportunity for us to step into the big leagues with a blue-chip consumer account. We ended up winning the account, but quickly felt the burn of the service demands that the account required. The account was incredibly demanding and required significantly more resources than we had allocated. We probably should have gone out and hired specialists just to service the account. However, the fee the client was paying us simply didn't enable us to staff the account appropriately. The client should have paid us three to four times more than the original fee so that we could adequately service the account.

The truth is, I underquoted them in the pricing process.

All of this could have been avoided if I had asked a simple question: "What is your budget?"

I was too afraid to ask the client this simple question because I was concerned it would delay the selection process and jeopardize our chances of winning the account. Not asking that question was a huge mistake. It ended up costing us valuable time, resources and opportunity, and we compromised the service experience for the client as a result. If I had just asked the simple question, chances are the client would have given us whatever budget we wanted in order to adequately service the account.

When it comes to career outcomes, you want to take clear and measurable steps in order to hit your big goals. These outcomes don't come from guesswork — they come from understanding exactly what is required of you to get the job done. If you don't ask, you'll never know.

Don't let shyness, laziness or fear of how people will respond deter you. Ask the question. Get your answer. Do what is asked. That's a winning formula right there.

Don't be afraid to ask. Questions are not for the weak of heart.

LESSON #92: MANAGE TO AN OUTCOME, NOT TO A MESSAGE

One of my biggest shortcomings over the years has been my tendency to manage to a message. Many times, I've made mistakes by managing simply to send a message or to prove a point to someone, when in reality I knew what the answer or the solution was. Rather than telling someone the answer or offering a solution, I've let the person fend for themselves, knowing that the outcome would be negative.

Back in the early days of my career, I thought this was a good management approach.

"How can your people get better if they don't figure it out on their own?" I used to ask myself.

That was a big mistake. As a manager, you should always *manage to an outcome, not to a message.*

I can remember many examples where I left a lot to be desired in this area. Most of these mistakes tend to happen around people and processes.

One of the people examples happened in 2017, when we were adding a new junior service team representative to our account management operation. It was evident to me right away that our hiring manager got the hire wrong. The manager was new to hiring and didn't take the necessary steps to vet the qualifications, experience and cultural fit of the candidate. We didn't have a dedicated talent development function at the time, and we clearly didn't give the manager the proper training or tools he needed in order to be effective at making hiring decisions.

The end result was that we hired the wrong person for the job. The candidate we hired was a perfect storm of poor talent, attitude and work ethic — the worst possible combination. I knew we got the hire wrong immediately. However, rather than tell the hiring manager *why* he got the hire wrong and *how* to fix it, I let him fend for himself. I kept my mouth shut and watched the situation crash and burn right before my eyes.

By the time the hiring manager came to us with a recommendation to terminate the employee, the damage had already been done. We lost a few important client accounts and we lost some well-liked and high-performing employees who didn't want to be in an environment with the toxic employee.

Had I just managed to an *outcome* instead of a *message*, we would have cut our losses quickly, replaced the bad employee with a better one, and retained a few important clients and employees along the way.

One of the process examples happened in 2012. We had just upgraded our healthcare plan, expanded our benefits offering, and added a new 401(k) and vision care program in order to attract more senior talent to our management team. During this time, we implemented a new human resource process to manage employee enrollment and help us allocate the appropriate benefits-related expenses in our budget.

One of the managers we recruited was impressed by the benefits package. This person ended up coming to work for our firm, in large part due to the benefits we offered. This hire was incredibly talented but had little regard for the process we put in place for enrolling in our program. Although the person had been instructed in the onboarding process how to enroll in our program, he completely disregarded the process soon after. Rather than reminding him about proper enrollment protocol, I didn't say anything, and he ended up missing his enrollment window. He was furious and ended up quitting.

This is another perfect example of managing to a message instead of managing to an outcome. To prove a point to the employee, I was too stubborn to remind him about the proper protocol because it was clearly explained during the onboarding process. The end result was that we lost a talented senior manager and our client service dropped significantly until we found a replacement. That was not a positive outcome by any means.

You don't get any bonus points for being able to say "I told you so." All you get is a losing outcome.

As a manager, you're going to be evaluated based on results and outcomes, not on messages. You should apply this in your day-to-day management approach and practices.

Always manage to an outcome, not to a message. Take it from someone who has learned this the hard way.

LESSON #93: MUTE THE NOISE

A few years ago, I made a commitment that changed my career forever. For this lesson, I am reminded of the great Teddy Roosevelt quote about the "Man in the Arena":

"It is not the critic who counts, not the man who points out how the strong man stumbles…it is the man who is actually in the arena, whose face is marred by dust, sweat and blood."

The early part of my business career was defined by the "critic," as Roosevelt would say, as much as it was by the "man in the arena." In other words, negative energy was just as prevalent as positive energy.

When I wanted to accomplish something ambitious, people would tell me why I *couldn't* do it as opposed to why I *could* do it. When I made poor decisions, people would laugh at my management skills, my leadership abilities or poke holes through my strategy. Whenever I experienced success, people were jealous in one way or another, whether it was because of financial gain, our business growth or the accomplishments of those who had helped us scale through the years. People would take shots by questioning my intelligence, criticizing our business or doubting our people in some way.

This negative energy had a big impact during the formative years of our business. While it motivated me to prove people wrong, it also created an unhealthy sense of paranoia, fear and doubt in many of the decisions that I made. I tried not to let it impact my confidence or decision-making abilities, but it rattled my psyche at times. I spent many nights staring at the ceiling and questioning if these people were right. Perhaps the career journey I chose was the wrong one.

In time, I discovered that most if not all of this negative energy was driven by the insecurity of *others*, not by my own insecurity. The negative energy was driven by the jealousy and self-doubt of haters who were quick to criticize but slow to come up with solutions of their own. They were the first to take shots but the last to step into the "arena." As you're reading this, I'm sure you can think of many people in your own career who fit this description.

I found that all this negative energy was nothing more than a huge distraction. It was impacting my decision-making and the sense of enjoyment I was getting out of my job, and it was hurting our people as a result.

It was nothing more than noise, so I made a commitment to *mute the noise*.

My career changed for the better. I had built a stable of great people who believed in me, and whose presence I enjoyed. We had so many great things to offer as a company, and we had a line of people who wanted to be a part of it. I realized how many great things I had going for me and how many great people I had around me. We had built something truly special, and I was allowing the noise around me to impact building something even *more* special.

By *muting the noise*, I made a conscious decision not to let any outside distractions get in my way. I refused to let the *noise* impede my ability to grow, improve, and become the best manager and leader I could be for the people who wanted to be there with me.

I put my head down and started to run our business without letting any distractions get in the way. I asked everyone in our company and everyone in my career who believed in me to hold me accountable for *muting the noise*, and I asked them to do the same for themselves. I wasn't going to let myself or the people I believed in get distracted, demoralized or defeated by any outside noise in their careers.

Ever since I made the decision to *mute the noise,* my career and business has been better off. Today, I make decisions based only on what the right decision is, not which decision will create the least amount of noise on the outside. I choose to surround myself with only those who bring positive energy. I choose to work with only those who pull in the direction of the same goal, not *against* the goal. Today, my job is much more enjoyable, healthy and productive than it's ever been.

Muting the noise was the best decision I ever made.

Surround yourself with positive energy, great people and those who want to share in your success, not criticize it. Don't let any outside distractions get in your head.

If there's noise in your career — and I'm sure there is — *mute it*.

LESSON #94: THE COST OF PEOPLE MISTAKES

I estimate that around 90 percent of all the mistakes I've made over the past decade can be categorized in one of the following buckets:

People I *hired.*

People I *fired.*

People I *didn't hire.*

People I *didn't fire.*

What is the common thread in all this?

People.

Most of the mistakes I've made in my career have to do with *people*. They have to do with the decisions that I've made regarding people, and then how I've handled myself with those people after the decisions were made. My biggest mistakes, regrets and learnings have all come from this area. I've made too many people mistakes to count.

The most important point is, people mistakes will cost you, and they'll cost you *big*. Between time, money and lost opportunity, the cost of people mistakes is almost incalculable. However, using a hypothetical example, I wanted to share just how much one people mistake could cost you.

Let's chalk this example up to the *People I hired* bucket.

You've just hired a new manager named Rino to join your team. Between his base salary, benefits and bonus, let's say Rino costs you $125,000 in total compensation. One month after you hire him, it becomes evident that Rino is not working out. Rather than move on from Rino immediately, you put him on a performance-improvement plan and agree to evaluate him in 60 days. After 60 days pass, he still isn't working out, so you terminate him.

You've already cost yourself approximately $30,000 in salary alone. Plus, between meetings with Rino, review sessions, checkpoints and correcting his mistakes, you've probably spent somewhere around 30 hours of your valuable time dealing with the problem. Let's say the value of your time to your company is $150 per hour. The Rino mistake is already at $34,500 just 90 days in.

Now the search for Rino's replacement is underway. This involves your recruiter's time plus sufficient budget to repost job ads. You spend another 60 days searching and interviewing, and ultimately hiring a replacement. Between the value of your recruiter's time, the cost of job ads, plus the additional time you've had to spend interviewing candidates, you've probably added another 50 hours of time, or somewhere in the neighborhood of $10,000 in additional lost opportunity costs. The Rino mistake is already up to almost $45,000, 80 hours, and has required involvement from yourself, human resources and finance, and his replacement hasn't even started yet. You also have to pull in your human resources person to onboard, train and process paperwork for the replacement, so you've now caused that person to do twice the amount of work he would have otherwise done. That probably means he's not happy with you, and you can expect to get the cold shoulder next time you have questions about your 401(k) contributions.

On top of all this, there's likely been a ripple effect across the entire organization. Because of Rino's underperformance, your highest quality resources were probably forced to pick up for his slack. This caused one or two of them to leave your company. Now you have to go back to the drawing board and find their replacements on top of Rino's replacement. That alone added another 30 hours of time, or $10,000 in value, from you and the recruiter.

Wait, there's more. Since there was a gap between Rino and his replacement, you likely lost two customers as a result. Let's say the average annual customer value is $100,000. You've now cost the company an extra $200,000. Now you need to pull in the sales team to go find new customers to replace the lost revenue that came as a result of Rino.

I've lost track of the tab at this point, but it's somewhere around $400,000 in value, 100 hours of time, and countless more in lost opportunity costs. The Rino mistake has impacted every layer of the org chart, from entry-level to executive level, and it has impacted every department and function within the organization, including service, sales, human resources and recruiting. Not to mention all the intangible costs to the organization, such as staff morale, reputational impact and infrastructure disruption.

The best part? Rino's replacement hasn't even started yet! Imagine if the replacement doesn't work out, a highly possible scenario considering that this person will be inheriting the mess Rino left behind — unhappy customers, unhappy subordinates and a team in disarray. If the replacement doesn't work out, you'll have to go through the exercise all over again, painful step by painful step.

I realize this is a mind-numbing exercise, but that's *exactly* the point. The cost of people mistakes is incalculable. Between hard costs, opportunity costs and intangible costs, people mistakes will set you back more than any other mistake you can make in your career.

When it comes to people, do everything you can to get these decisions right. Go slowly if you have to. Pull in other people for their perspectives. Do whatever it takes so you don't make the Rino mistake again.

LESSON #95: NEW YORK, NEW YORK

This lesson is going to sound haughty. I'm probably going to turn off my many friends, clients and peers across the world. I'm sorry for that, but it needs to be said.

There is *no* place like New York when it comes to business.

This is my business love song to New York.

I've traveled to more than 100 cities and four continents in the 10 years since I started our business. I've been to trade shows in more than 30 cities. I've attended client events in more than 20 states. I've networked with businesspeople in more than a dozen state capitals.

I've *transacted, interacted, eaten, listened, walked, exercised, conversed, argued, laughed, explored*, and done everything else you could possibly think of, in some of the greatest places in the world. I've met with clients at the Fisherman's Wharf in San Francisco, I've eaten deep dish pizza with prospects in Chicago, I've been told to get lost by a vendor in Washington, D.C., I've networked with peers at events under the San Diego sun, and I've toasted with technologists on the Boston Harbor.

All of these places are nice, but there's *no* place like New York.

The energy of New York City is unique. Its electricity is ideal for being an entrepreneur or an ambitious, career-minded professional. If you take advantage of it, the city will push, challenge and motivate you to become the best version of your professional self.

New York is a challenging place to survive, but if you can win in business here, it's the most rewarding place you as a professional can call home. There is a pace, grittiness and toughness to New York that doesn't exist anywhere else.

The city has served as the perfect backdrop for my career and for our business. It has become as much a character in the cast of our company as any individual. I can't imagine that we would have experienced the same levels of success or progress if we had chosen another city to call home.

Beyond the energy and electricity that the city offers, it also offers opportunity like no place else. New York has offered access to networking contacts, events and informational resources that have helped me get ahead in my career.

Rather than treat clients, prospects and co-workers to *good* food, New York lets you treat them to the *best* food, and from anywhere in the world.

You have access to wealth, poverty, culture, diversity and cuisine, all within a short subway ride.

You have access to the greatest talent pool in the world. People travel from all over the world to give their careers a go in New York.

You have access to the best that the fields of finance, real estate, art and media have to offer.

You have places to go when you need peace and tranquility. You have places to go when you need speed and expediency.

My point is that, all the resources and tools that New York has to offer can be invaluable to you on your career journey. If you're working in New York, you're not doing your career any justice unless you're taking full advantage of the resources the city has to offer.

New York might not have the *specialization* that other cities have, but it has *diversification* that no other city can offer. San Francisco has technology, Milan has fashion, Houston has oil, but New York has *everything*. When it comes to your career, you want as much of *everything* as you can get. You want as much diversity, information and access as possible. No other city in the world can offer this like New York can.

New York, New York. Sorry, friends. When it comes to business, there's *no* place like New York.

I hope you enjoyed my business love song to the *greatest* city in the world.

LESSON #96: THE DIFFERENCE BETWEEN MANAGEMENT AND LEADERSHIP

Management and leadership often get unfairly lumped together. However, the two are very different.

The tricky part about being an entrepreneur is that you must wear both hats at different times. Sometimes entrepreneurship calls for you to be a strong manager, and at other times it requires that you're a strong leader. Some of the biggest lessons that I've learned have been when I confused the two.

Whenever I've worn the manager hat when our people needed me to be a leader, I've made some of the biggest mistakes in leadership. Conversely, whenever I've worn the leader hat when our people needed me to manage properly, I've made some of the biggest mistakes in management.

I've studied management versus leadership extensively over the past 10 years as I've tried to improve in both areas. Ultimately, I believe the fundamental difference between management and leadership boils down to the "potential" rule.

Great managers get their people to *reach* their potential, while great leaders get their people to reach *beyond* their potential.

Strong management is all about diligence, organization and efficiency. Most good managers with whom I've worked have been fast-moving pragmatists. They work quickly but they work intelligently. They tend to live in the "now" rather than in the future. Their approach is typically rooted in optimizing the efficiencies of their people. They are competent in the areas of goal setting, follow through and resource distribution. They hold people accountable for meeting deadlines, setting expectations and hitting their key performance indicators (KPIs).

Other traits that I've noticed strong managers possess include a clear and concise approach to communication, fair and balanced reasoning skills, acute attention to detail, and a high degree of intellect. All of these skills point toward resource optimization, and thus, I've learned that good managers will get their people to *reach* their potential.

On the other hand, strong leadership is all about intangibles. The best leaders I've been around have been the ones with the highest emotional quotient (EQ) and can relate to their people through humility, empathy and empowerment. In their dealings with people, they live just as much in the future as in the present. They are constantly showing their people where they believe they *can* go rather than showing them where they are going in the moment. Thus, I've learned that good leaders will get their people to reach *beyond* their potential.

I've found that strong leaders are stimulating communicators, using their communication skills as a way to stimulate. While strong managers display balanced reasoning, sometimes strong leaders possess unbalanced reasoning and set expectations that are unreasonable.

Most importantly, I've noticed that leadership comes down to strong integrity, humility and an ability to admit mistakes. While strong management skills point toward resource optimization, strong leadership skills point toward resource *acceleration*.

I've struggled to figure out whether leadership is a skill that can be *acquired* or if it's a quality that is *inherited*. I've gained exposure to so many different types of great corporate leaders over the years. I've also been exposed to some of the worst leaders and pacesetters who have destroyed perfectly innovative companies that otherwise would have grown.

I've studied the patterns and commonalities between the two and found that most good leaders have an inherent ability to lead. While it can be improved in time, most of these leaders have had natural abilities that are difficult to acquire. This hasn't been the case with all the great leaders I've come across, but the majority have possessed a natural ability to lead.

The best managers, on the other hand, have not necessarily been born with strong management skills. The best managers are the ones who developed management skills, and improved these skills with constant repetition, rigor and analytics. The best managers weren't born with natural management abilities, they *worked* their way to the top.

I've used the "potential" rule to guide my decisions whenever I have evaluated whether to hire a manager versus a leader. If you think back to the managers and leaders you've been exposed to over your career, I believe you'll find that the best managers got you to *reach* your potential, but the best leaders got you to reach *beyond* your potential.

LESSON #97: TURN TO THE OUTSIDE FOR FIRST-TIME HIRES

One of my favorite parts of growing a business over the past decade has been the opportunity to create new positions within the company. As our business has grown, so has the necessity to add new departments and functions, including sales, finance, human resources, operations and IT. Creating these new opportunities and adding new dimensions to the organization has been one of the most rewarding parts of growing a business.

When it comes to hiring for new positions, I've learned that you don't know what you don't know. It's always best to seek outside counsel and listen to people who have hired these positions before.

In 2017, we were finally ready to hire a Chief Financial Officer. Our business had grown to a point where we needed a seasoned senior financial professional to bring our finance function to the next level. Up until that point, our finance function was managed by our head of operations, who also ran human resources and served as a general manager for all office operations. He did a fine job managing all these tasks, but we had grown to a point where we needed to add a dedicated role to bring new processes, discipline and strategy to our finance function.

I had no background in finance and my only real exposure to finance was a crash course in basic budgeting, forecasting and balance sheet evaluations that I had received over the years since starting the business. At that point, I had experience hiring sales, service, management and operations positions, but I had never made a finance hire before, especially one at a senior level. I had no clue what I was doing, what to look for or who to hire.

The first call I made was to Mike White. Mike was the former CFO of PepsiCo who went on to become CEO of DirecTV. He had an incredible pedigree, having run finance under legendary CEO Roger Enrico at PepsiCo, as well as leading DirecTV through one of the most historic mergers ever with AT&T. I was introduced to Mike through a mutual acquaintance a few years earlier, and he was gracious enough to agree to meet with me over dinner on the Upper East Side of Manhattan. I developed a great rapport with Mike over the years. He became a mentor and an invaluable resource for whenever I needed help. This was clearly one of those times.

Mike helped me contextualize the traits I needed in my finance hire. First off, I was running a small business that was morphing into a midsized business, so I didn't need a PepsiCo-level CFO who was used to working with unlimited resources. Rather, I needed somebody who would be willing to roll up his or her sleeves and be independent. At the same time, hiring someone with a large company background and who possessed strong corporate discipline could serve me well, Mike explained.

This helped me narrow my search and identify the appropriate persona of the ideal finance candidate. The candidate would need to have a blend of corporate experience to go along with some roll-up-your sleeves ability that is crucial in a smaller entrepreneurial setting. The candidate needed to be strong in strategy and analytics, but equally as competent in finance administration. Most importantly, the candidate needed to be a good cultural fit, and couldn't rub his or her nose when asked to perform mundane daily financial tasks such as expense reports, QuickBooks reconciliations and spreadsheet maintenance.

I then worked with outside people who I trusted, such as my father and some of my clients who had financial backgrounds, to put together an interview process with three stages. The first stage included an introductory screening, followed by an in-person committee meeting the candidate agreed to take part in, and finally a presentation and a chemistry check that I was a part of. At each step of the way, I leaned on outside support to make sure that I was equipped with the right questions and that I understood what traits to look for.

Finally, in the fall of 2017 we hired Jim Morris from JPMorgan Chase. He had the perfect background for us and turned out to be one of the best hires I've ever made. He got our finance function to the next level by implementing new reporting structures and analytics, he helped me on expense management and worked side-by-side with me to help me improve my own financial acumen. He built the financial models for our employee rewards programs, he implemented tools to understand client and staff profitability, and he developed pricing models that optimized our revenue. Most importantly, he was a great culture fit, an even better man, and has become a trusted member of the team.

When it comes to making first-time hires, I learned to put my ego aside. By turning to the outside for advice, counsel and perspectives, you'll be better off for it on the inside.

LESSON #98: DON'T DISCRIMINAGE

I've learned that age diversity in the workplace is among the most critically important components to improving company culture. Whenever we've had demographics that cut across many age groups and generational categories, I've found that our innovation, morale and camaraderie has benefitted tremendously.

We've had a diversity in our perspectives that contributed tremendously to our growth whenever we were the most age diversified. Conversely, whenever our age diversity has been narrowest, our culture has suffered. Oftentimes, this has resulted in stagnation, lack of innovation and poor employee morale.

However, I've learned not to have any preconceived notions about a candidate based on his or her age or experience levels. Some of the most mature and responsible displays of professionalism over the years have come from our youngest employees. I can remember many times when an entry-level employee or intern shocked me with acts of empathy, compassion and maturity. Conversely, some of the most petty and adolescent displays have come from our oldest employees. I can remember many times when I was flabbergasted by the poor leadership, insubordination and immaturity displayed by senior employees.

The big challenge is trying to figure out how to achieve proper age diversity without being predisposed to a given candidate based on the number of years on his or her resume. As I've learned through the years, you should look for *age-agnostic* qualities when evaluating candidates. This is usually a safe bet and will bring greater diversity and harmony to your team.

I've learned that when you start recruiting for specific *qualities* rather than *experience* levels, you'll start to build a well-rounded culture. Most importantly, you'll start to build a culture that displays 360-degree diversity — meaning diversity across all demographics, backgrounds and perspectives. This will enrich your team by ensuring that your culture is constantly in improvement mode, and that it is viewed as an unfinished canvas that requires contributions and perspectives from all.

Cultural innovation and improvement are not driven by years on a resume. Instead, they are driven by qualities and traits that are *age-agnostic*.

Here are some of the qualities and traits that I've found to cut across all generations and age brackets:

Positive energy. Someone who displays authentic optimism, not contrived or phony optimism.

A global perspective. Someone who views a job with a global mindset, not a provincial one.

An intellectually experimental mindset. Someone who is stimulated through experimentation and wants to try new things out.

An insatiable appetite to learn. Someone who can never get enough access to information and is on a constant mission to learn.

A vision for the future. Someone who has a clear vision for himself or herself in the future and who doesn't live in the past.

People junkies. Someone who enjoys being around people and is not afraid to get up and walk around the office.

Servant leaders. Someone who leads others through service and acts versus words.

A studious mindset. Someone who views himself or herself as a student just as much as a teacher.

Someone who has been on a team before. Someone who has participated in a team-oriented activity or sport before.

A player/coach. Someone who can focus on both tactics and execution.

In my dealings managing people in the workplace, I've learned that these are *age-agnostic* qualities. They apply to all generations, age groups and experience levels. I would encourage you to recruit with an age-agnostic eye. This will lead you to find can't-miss talent that cuts across all generations.

Don't *discriminAGE* in the workplace. Always be on the lookout for candidates who display age-agnostic qualities and your culture will be better off as a result.

LESSON #99: UNICORNS AND CLYDESDALES

I never thought that *making* money would be a penalty until I started running a business. Read that sentence again. You're probably scratching your head. Don't worry, I'm still scratching my head about it 10 years later.

In 2015, our revenues were hovering at around $5 million, we had taken no outside capital, and we had been profitable every year since the company was founded. We might not have been Google, but we had built a profitable business. We had done it all with our own sweat and blood, and we had a track record of five years of profitability and growth. We had built a damn good small business, and I was proud of that.

An investor who had backed several of our start-up technology clients was flying in from San Francisco and wanted to catch up with me over dinner to discuss the performance of his portfolio. I met him at the Tribeca Grill in downtown Manhattan. As soon as we sat down, he started raving about how well his technology portfolio companies were performing.

"This company just raised a $30 million Series B round," he boasted. "This one has a valuation of $200 million." Naturally, I applauded him and complimented him on his vision to invest in these companies early.

"This one is going to go public in two years, I can feel it!" he exclaimed. "And this one is a *unicorn*!"

It was the first time that I had heard the word *unicorn* used in a business context. Little did I know that in the years ahead, it would become an everyday term used to describe red-hot start-ups with ungodly valuations.

After listening to him laud the brilliance of his investing vision and the performance of his portfolio, I asked him a logical question.

"Which one of them is making the most money?" I asked.

He started laughing, almost uncontrollably. I didn't understand why he was laughing. I thought it might have been because my fly was unzipped or because I had something stuck in my teeth, so I excused myself and headed for the restroom. As I made my way down the legendary corridor in the Tribeca Grill with photos featuring Robert DeNiro and other New York icons, I was puzzled by what had just happened at the table.

Why was this guy laughing at me? I wondered.

As soon as I had collected myself and returned to dinner, I asked him what was so funny.

"None of these companies make money, Matt," he told me. "If you asked that question in San Francisco they'd look at you like you were crazy."

He went on to explain how the business models worked for these *unicorns*. They constantly focused on growth, exploited all opportunities to disrupt an industry, and rarely worried about profitability. It was a totally new concept to me when I heard it for the first time. All I had known over the past five years was hard work, calculated risk taking and how to stay focused on growth but maintain profitability. That was the only business formula I knew.

He then asked me how my business was doing. I explained to him that we were growing 15 to 20 percent consistently year over year, we had healthy profit margins, we were making money, we were hiring new people, and we were reinvesting our own capital back into the business to grow.

"Good for you, Matt," he said. "You have built a great lifestyle business."

He said it in a condescending way, just like he was talking to a kindergartner who had done something cute.

Lifestyle business. This was another word that I was hearing for the first time.

What the hell is a "lifestyle business"? I thought.

Later, I would learn what it was — a business that is set up to generate a certain level of income and focus on maintaining profitability.

There I was, a young entrepreneur, working my ass off, trying to do things the right way, and running a healthy, profitable business each and every year. Yet, in some weird, twisted way, that was somehow a *bad* thing.

"How could I be penalized for doing things the *right* way?" I asked myself.

Over the years, I've seen great start-up companies turn into true unicorns. Some of these are start-ups that I've had the privilege of representing and whose founders, CEOs and board members I've developed great relationships with. I've also seen so-called unicorns crash and burn and represent the epitome of greed, hubris and the exploitation of capitalism. Companies like WeWork and Theranos. If these companies are a breed of unicorns, then companies like mine are Clydesdales: hard-working and reliable, constantly pulling the wagon, and full of vitality.

A decade later, I'm very comfortable with what we've built. We might never be a unicorn, but we're a damn good business. I don't care what it's called, whether it's a lifestyle business or something else.

Here's to all the Clydesdales out there. Be *proud* of what you've built.

LESSON #100: 90 PERCENT HEART, 10 PERCENT HEAD

The final lesson I want to share is one that I've found to be true no matter where you are along your career journey or in the org chart. Most importantly, this is a lesson that is fully within your control no matter what background, credentials or years of experience you have.

Success in your career is *90 percent heart, 10 percent head.*

I may be of modest intelligence compared to other men and women who run companies, but I have an insatiable work ethic and a burning passion for what I do. I've learned to use the office as a ball field and leave everything I have on the field. Whatever I may lack in the way of brains, I overcompensate for with my heart. I've found this to be a successful formula, and one that has proven I can accomplish things an IQ test would indicate I could never dream of accomplishing.

If success in your career is defined by progress and reaching your potential, then you're going to have use your *heart* over your head to get there.

I've met so many people over the years with superior intelligence, impressive academic pedigrees and formidable credentials. Their minds work in ways that mine never could. Many of them could have gone on to achieve truly great things in their careers, but their lack of desire and passion and their low threshold for sacrifice inhibited them from reaching their potential. They are examples of smart failures. They possess an intelligence far greater than mine, but they lack the heart that I have. They have the brains to accomplish great things — much greater things than I have — and yet, their lack of heart has cost them.

Most examples of untapped potential that I've come across in my career have had to do with problems of the heart, not of the head — shortcomings in regard to complacency and work ethic, overt displays of hubris and condescension, and issues with integrity and character. These are all examples of traits that I've seen destroy and derail companies and careers that otherwise had tremendous potential.

You should always choose *heart* over *head* in your career. It will lead you to good places and it will get you closer to reaching your potential.

At the beginning of 2020, we set the most ambitious goal we ever set as a company. To kick off the year, I held an all-hands meeting with our staff, as I've done for the past 10 years. The prior year was not a great year. We didn't reach our potential, and I felt that it happened primarily because we leaned on our head over our heart. We overthought and overanalyzed, and lost a glimmer of the fighting spirit that enabled us to build a great company in the first place.

I turned to my team and told them that the theme of the year would be *90 percent heart, 10 percent head*. I asked everyone to take this mindset with them as they approached their jobs every day. I asked them to put themselves out there, to show their passion and to be comfortable taking risks. Everyone made a commitment to show their heart for the whole year.

I didn't want to look back at the year with any regret, wondering what could have been if we had only shown more heart than we did. At this writing, the year is still in progress, so we'll see how it ends up. If history is any indication, we'll be just fine.

I've learned that the *heart over head* mindset applies to everyone in their careers, no matter where a person is on his or her journey. Everyone has a different intellect, but we all have the same ability to show our heart. You're in full control of whether you show your heart.

You can live with failure as a result of not having the intellectual capacity to do something, but you can't live with failure because you didn't have the heart to do something.

You can only give 100 percent in your career. You can't give any more than that. It's up to you to make the call on how you want to split it up. I know how I'll always choose to split mine up.

90 percent heart, 10 percent head.

That's my split. It might not make you the most intelligent version of yourself, but it is a guaranteed formula to make you the most successful version of yourself.

CLOSING: "BET ON WALL"

I hope you enjoyed reading *Embrace the Pace: The 100 Most Exhilarating Lessons Learned in a Decade of Entrepreneurship.*

You now officially have a place on my "bet on" wall (remember that from "Lesson #29: Make Someone Proud, Prove Someone Wrong"?). By sharing in these lessons, it gives me great pleasure that you'll be joined with me as I embark on the next chapter of my career. Next time you're in downtown Manhattan, swing by our office so we can get a picture together and put it up on the "bet on" wall.

Similarly, I hope you know that you can count me as one of the many believers in your career and that you'll put me on your own version of your "bet on" wall or that you'll include me on your "make proud" list.

This book was one of the most enjoyable and cathartic experiences I've had over the past decade. It brought back so many memories of all kinds. Most importantly, it brought to mind all the great people who have helped to shape my career over the past decade, and all the valuable lessons that I've learned along the way. The experience of writing this book and sharing these lessons with you was truly exhilarating for me. I definitely "Embraced the Pace" in every sense.

I hope you can find a small place for these lessons somewhere in your career journey, no matter how far along you are. There is no feeling like sharing in the success of each other's careers. If I was able to share something that impacts your career journey in some small way through these lessons, then this book was a success as far as I'm concerned.

For me, the road to become one of the one percent of businesses that builds a global presence begins now. Whatever road you choose to pursue in your next chapter, please know that I'll be cheering for you.

Let's make a bet on each other and check back a decade from now. Hopefully, we can swap lessons and celebrate the achievement of beating the odds together.

Here's to the career journey. Here's to the beauty of your career. Here's to the beauty of learning.

#EmbraceThePace

THE "BET ON" WALL

A special thanks to everyone who has bet on me over the past decade. Your names are forever etched onto my "Bet On" wall. Also, a big thanks to everyone who has motivated me by making it onto my "Bet Against" wall. Let's get you onto the "Bet On" wall for the next chapter.

All my current and former N6A teammates

My wonderful family and friends

Aaron Kwittken

Al DiGuido

Alex Yampolskiy

Amy Holtzman

Ben Hindman

Brian Buchwald

Brian Rubin

Carolyn Knott

Charlie Bonello

Charlie Stephens

Chris Pellegrino

Craig Rosenberg

Daniela Mancinelli

David Goldin

David Kingsdale

David Sommer

David Reid

Dawn Short

Doug Jarvis

Eric Handa

Erich Joachimsthaler

Ezra Kucharz

Fatima Zaidi

Gary Chartrand

Geoff Judge

George King

Gil Beyda

Gil Eyal

Gino Bello

Giovanni DeMeo

Guy Poreh

Hadley Ford

Hunter Newby

Iona College Friends and Family

Jade Scipioni

James Barcia

James Lamberti

Jared Hardwick

Jason Fudin

Jim Fosina

Jim Morris

Joe's Pizza of Fleetwood Crew

John Hannaway

Jordan Cohen

Josh Mait

Judge Graham

Katherine Dillon

Kelly Short

Marc Poirier

Maria Ortiz

Mark Feldman

Mark Zamuner

Marketing EDGE Board Members and Team

Mary Beth Keelty

Micah Tapman

Michael Nyman

Michaelangelo

Mike Shields

Mike Sweetney

Mike White

Morgan Harris

Nick Junta

Nina Velasquez

Pascal Ehrsam

Pascal Kaufmann

Pete Rogers

Phil Palazzo

Ravneet Bhandari

Rick Martira

Rob May

Roshni Wijayasinha

Sanjay Chadda

Sean Carney

Scott Albro

Scott Galloway

Stephen Bradley

Steve Gershik

Steve Sarracino

Steve Weiss

Stuart Elliott

Suneet Bhatt

The Al's Angels Family

The Boldstart Ventures Team

The Camber Creek Team

The CI Capital Team

The MediaLink Team

The Primary Ventures Team

The Propeller Group Team

The Shea Brothers

The Staudt Family

The Stephens Group

Tony Case

Tony Ibrahim

Trace Smith

Travis Jarae

Vin Beni

Wendy Haig

LESSONS TABLE MATRIX

LESSON LEARNED	LESSON #
Entrepreneurship	*1, 2, 16, 33, 35, 40, 46, 85, 99*
Professional Development	*3, 4, 7, 12, 66, 70, 71, 72, 87*
Leadership	*5, 21, 69, 73, 76, 96*
General Career Lessons	*6, 8, 13, 23, 26, 28, 34, 37, 42, 48, 53, 62, 67, 93, 100*
Culture	*9, 11, 14, 50, 64, 82, 88, 95*
Management	*10, 19, 20, 30, 36, 38, 45, 49, 54, 56, 58, 60, 63, 68, 79, 92*
Hiring	*15, 39, 52, 55, 94, 97, 98*
Sales	*17, 65, 86, 91*
Marketing	*18, 83*
Innovation	*22, 32, 44*
Customer Service	*24, 25, 59, 75, 84, 89*
Competition	*27, 31, 41, 77*
Family	*29, 43, 47, 78, 90*
Risk	*51, 81*
Finance	*57, 61, 74, 80*

END NOTES

Certain parts of *Embrace the Pace: The 100 Most Exhilarating Lessons Learned in a Decade of Entrepreneurship* are works of the author previously published in the following articles:

Lesson #15: "The Betting Game" https://www.entrepreneur.com/article/302283

Lesson #18: "Youth is a Differentiator" https://www.entrepreneur.com/article/319603

Lesson #43: "Lessons from Mom" https://www.almostmillions.com/2017/05/12/five-mothers-day-entrepreneurial-lessons/

Lesson #47: "Find a Safe Haven in Your Career" https://westfaironline.com/101797/matt-rizzetta-for-mount-vernon-it-all-starts-with-leadership/

Lesson #98: "Don't DiscriminAGE" https://thebossmagazine.com/age-diversity/

FOOTNOTE CITATIONS

1. https://www.pmi.org/-/media/pmi/documents/public/pdf/learning/thought-leadership/why-good-strategies-fail-report.pdf
2. https://hbr.org/2017/11/executives-fail-to-execute-strategy-because-theyre-too-internally-focused
3. https://onlinelibrary.wiley.com/doi/abs/10.1111/j.1559-1816.2002.tb00216.x